CHILDREN'S CHAMPION

CHILDREN'S CHAMPION

THE STORY OF NIGEL WILLIAMS

Lynda Neilands

Foreword by Alf McCreary

COLOURPOINT

*To Aneurin
and future grandchildren*

© Lynda Neilands and Colourpoint Books, 2009

ISBN: 978 1 906578 17 6

First Edition
First Impression

Design by April Sky Design, Newtownards
Printed by CPI Cox and Wyman, Reading

Colourpoint Books
Colourpoint House
Jubilee Business Park
21 Jubilee Road
Newtownards
County Down
Northern Ireland
BT23 4YH

Tel: 028 9182 6339
Fax: 028 9182 1900
E-mail: info@colourpoint.co.uk
Web site: www.colourpoint.co.uk

About the Author
Teacher, writer and storyteller, **Lynda Neilands** grew up in Portadown. Like Nigel, she attended Portadown College, playing Jessica to his Shylock in a memorable school production of *The Merchant of Venice*. She went on to read English and French in Trinity College, Dublin. Lynda now lives in Belfast where she teaches modern languages and creative communication. Her published work includes two ghost-written biographies and three popular volumes of stories for telling to children. In her leisure time she enjoys dog-walking in Botanic Gardens and drinking coffee in the Student's Union at Queen's.

Alf McCreary is Religion Correspondent of the Belfast Telegraph, and the author of a very wide range of books, including the acclaimed biographies of Lord Eames and the late Senator Gordon Wilson.

CONTENTS

FOREWORD

FROM MY PROFESSIONAL EXPERIENCE, one of the most difficult tasks facing any writer is to embark on a biography of another human being and to do justice to that person whose life is being portrayed, with all its lights and shades.

This is all the more difficult for an author when he or she is asked to write the biography by the subject who knows that he has a terminal illness. Given that particular challenge, Lynda Neilands has provided a broadbrush picture of a complex individual, and yet with enough detail to underline his many human qualities and his deep Christian faith. She has done so with affection but without undue sentimentality, and she allows the reader to make up his or her own mind about the real Nigel Williams.

It was not my privilege to have met Nigel in person, though I was aware of his key appointment in 2003 as Northern Ireland's first Commissioner for Children. However, I soon discovered that the man I encountered in this book had used his gifts and talents to maximum effect in helping other people, and particularly children.

One of Lynda Neiland's motives in writing this book was to help Nigel to fulfil his ambition to leave behind a record of events in his life which would encourage people, and especially those on a career ladder, to live out their faith in the real world.

Nigel William's faith was strong, but in many ways it was also unconventional. He was, as a friend remarked a "churchman without walls", and his religious journey included various periods in the Methodist Church, the inter-denominational and charismatic Belfast Christian Family, then Anglicanism in England, and finally in Cairncastle Presbyterian Church, back in Northern Ireland.

Early in the book, the author notes that "Nigel saw no need to reinvent himself" in terms of how he spoke, what he believed, what he did and how he went about it. This reminds me of some early and invaluable advice given to me by my first, and immensely distinguished, editor who said that some of the best writing is "an endless variation on an obvious theme."

This perhaps summarises best the life of Nigel Williams – an endless and creative series of variations, but the central theme was the practical out-working of Christianity itself, and its impact, for good, on individuals and communities.

Nigel Williams achieved this, but one of the great – and unanswered questions – about his life and untimely death is why 'bad' things happen to 'good' people.

It is beyond our comprehension to understand why Nigel Williams' life was cut short at the height of his achievements and during one of the most important periods of his life. One of the comforts, however, is to realise that he had used his talents to the full, and that in the best possible and New Testament sense he could say "I have fought a good fight, I have finished my course, I have kept the faith."

Lynda Neiland's biography is a fitting tribute to a remarkable life, which was lived with courage and conviction.

Alf McCreary MBE

PROLOGUE

THE ALARM WENT OFF, waking me from an uneasy doze. With a heavy heart, I threw off the bedclothes. All night long a sad little question had nagged at the back of my mind.

What do you say to a friend who is dying?

"He wants to write." Heather had told me on the phone. "He wondered if you would come and chat to him about it?"

I'd said 'yes' of course. But what sort of a chat would it be? What sort of writing did Nigel have in mind? He'd written some poetry, I knew. The trouble was that whatever he wrote, it couldn't be long – or more precisely, couldn't take long.

The thought, together with the sudden overnight drop in temperature, made me shiver. I opened the curtains to be greeted by white sentinel trees with starkly beautiful branches, guarding a carpet of snow. The street beyond the railings had a lethal sheen. Would this winter offensive put a stop to our plans? No. Before the sun had even begun to melt the ice, Nigel's daughter and her husband braved winding country roads to pick me up and transport me to Glenarm. I suppose deep down we all knew we couldn't afford to delay things. Barring a miracle Nigel had, at best, months to live.

Mission accomplished, Kathryn and Pete led the way into the muted warmth of the family home. Heather welcomed me with a hug. Still, I felt like an intruder. This was a time for intimate friends and relatives. Had it not been for Nigel's specific request, I would never have asked to visit him, and yet here I was being ushered up the stairs and into his room.

The first thing that struck me was the light. It streamed in through the glass of the bedroom window, its brilliance intensified by the snow-covered fields below. Nigel was seated in armchair. "Lynda, it's good of you to come." That was when I relaxed. Nigel had always had a way of putting people at their ease and today was no different. We'd last met at a party, nine months previously. Back then he'd described, with pride and enthusiasm, the display of photographic post cards created by his art student daughter for her final year exhibition at Manchester Metropolitan University. Today, apart from a hint of breathlessness and the red patterned rug draped across his legs, you wouldn't have known he was ill. That same glow of enthusiasm was in his eye – only this time the creative project he wanted to talk about was his own.

He had an idea for a book: not a poetry book, not a book of reflections. "What I have tried to do throughout my life," he explained, "is engage with God in a world that's messed up, to build his kingdom and bring change." The book would be based on his experiences, on lessons he had learnt and was keen to share; it would have something to say to younger people climbing the career ladder – something to say about key choices, about values, about decision-making.

Having outlined the idea, he relaxed and sipped his coffee. "So what do you think?"

I smiled back – comfortable in the role of creative writing tutor. "Great! I'd say go for it."

"There's just one problem," He gave me the characteristic Nigel look I remembered from our schooldays – a look of unusual directness, intensely serious yet with a hint of a twinkle in his eyes. "I'm not going to live long enough to do this – so I was just wondering, how would you feel about writing it for me?"

JANUARY 1995

WHERE TO START? In the long corridor of a life-history many key scenes leap out. "Begin here," they cry. "Recognise my central place in the record. Begin with me."

I settle for a scene on an aeroplane. A key scene, certainly. The key scene? Probably not. But it has sound effects (jet engines purring away in the background), dialogue (Nigel and Heather, making the most of a glorious stretch of uninterrupted companionship), and drama. Leona Lewis eat your heart out. How many married couples have "a moment like this', high above the clouds, away from the demands of jobs and children, sharing an idea that could change the course of their lives?

Nigel has been bursting to talk it over for days – rehearsing the conversation. He wants to explain things calmly and logically, so Heather understands exactly what he has in mind and why. But when it comes to the bit, the words just tumble out – "information superhighway"… "potential for growth"… "amazing opportunity"… "danger of computer pornography"… "protecting children."

"I feel I've got to do something about this," he finishes. "Raise funds, start a charity. I've been praying and praying and the idea just seems to get stronger." He squeezes her arm. "So what do you think?"

Heather meets his eyes, reading that familiar sparkle of excitement and drive. She trusts his spiritual judgement. She really wants to share his enthusiasm. Still her stomach churns.

"Nigel," she says bluntly, "Will it mean moving house?" For if it does, it will be the third major family upheaval in seven years.

CHAPTER ONE

A BORN LEADER

NIGEL FIRST MOVED HOUSE before birth.

It happened like this.

Tall precise Idwal Prichard Williams met chatty warm-hearted Phyllis Irene Ley (known as Rene) at a Methodist Guild Guest house in Scotland. She came from Devon. He came from Wales. He said to her, "You're very nice" (or words to that effect). She said to him, "I like you too". There followed a flurry of correspondence between Welshpool and Barnstaple and the consequence was they got married.

At that time Idwal held a position in the Valuation Office in Welshpool which meant the newly weds began their married life in Wales. There baby Sheila was born. But autumn 1954 brought the offer of a new job in the Valuation Division of the Department of Finance in Northern Ireland. Nigel's first move took place when Rene, pregnant for the second time, went back to live with her mother in Barnstaple until a suitable house in Ulster could be found.

So it came about that on 21 January 1955 Idwal returned to his digs in Londonderry to be greeted by a large placard proclaiming "It's a boy!"

"The District Valuer was most understanding," Idwal recalls, "and told me to go straight to Devon to see the new addition the family." He and Rene named the chubby, dark-haired baby Nigel Prichard.

Spring came and with it another move. The Williams family were united under the one Northern Irish roof – a Housing

Executive house in Limavady. A third move, in 1964, took the family (now a quintet since the birth of Nigel's second sister Sue) to their own home on the beautiful Roe Valley Estate.

—⁂—

Hold the thought of this new home by the river Roe. Another key scene beckons us into the future.

The setting is a conference room. Sound effects: the dull hum of city traffic. Nigel sits at a polished table with some work colleagues. The traffic can be heard because the room is silent. This is a different kind of conference – one where individuals take a trip back in time and confer with their memories. They have each been issued with a form asking them to review their life experiences. 'Think back to your childhood,' the opening question invites. 'Briefly describe something you enjoyed doing, believed you did well and that gave you a sense of satisfaction.'

A childhood achievement? Now the hum of the traffic overlays the racking of brains. These folk could easily evaluate what they've achieved in the last six weeks, six months, or even six years. But a *childhood* achievement? They frown and shift in their seats. Suddenly Nigel picks up his pen.

And he's away...

He sees a lone schoolboy striding along a leafy track, schoolbag bouncing on his shoulders. Companionably the river races alongside. Sunshine glints through the trees. The boy glimpses the blue dart of a kingfisher in the foliage and his dark eyes sparkle with a huge satisfaction. Yes, this is everything he hoped for – his best ever plan. How many kingfishers does he spot on his normal route to school? Breathe in, he tells himself. Let the achievement imprint itself on your memory. Inhale the fresh spring air. Outrun the excited tumble of the water. Fix your eyes on the bright open path ahead.

This memory springs from those days on the Roe Valley Estate. Each morning Nigel and his sisters walked along the Dungiven Road to Limavady Central Primary School. Idwal recollects that when he was ten Nigel wanted to go via the Country Park footpath. "His mother thought it too dangerous but, after much pleading, eventually agreed."

For Nigel the 'much pleading' had begun with a gentle hint. He liked maps and had worked out a route that would take him to school through the woods. "It would be great to walk that way." He made it sound like a casual observation. As the weeks went by the hints grew stronger. "I'd really like to walk to school through the woods." A few more weeks and he moved on to the vital question. "When can I walk to school through the woods?"

Rene was consulting a recipe book at the time and gave the sort of automatic answer that comes from having your mind elsewhere. "Probably when you're ten, dear" – whereupon a jubilant Nigel started computing the number of months, weeks and days until his birthday.

The birthday came and went with no reference to that conversation. Even at that early age Nigel knew the importance of timing. His goal seemed tantalisingly close but he had the emotional intelligence to know that no matter what his mother had said in the heat of a sponge-filled moment, she wasn't going to agree to him setting off along the river on a cold dark January morning. So he waited – waited for a spring morning when the sun shone, a morning when she wasn't under pressure, when Sheila and Susie were out of earshot, a morning when he could appear in the kitchen, bright and purposeful, with his school bag packed. "You said I could walk to school through the woods when I was ten, Mum." He made sure his voice sounded casual – as if it was no big deal. "So how about today?"

"*Today?* I'm not sure…"

"Why not, Mum?"

Briefly Rene searched for a convincing reason, but nothing suitable came to mind. "Oh, all right then," she sighed.

Often children and adults have very different perceptions of the same incident. While Idwal and Rene Williams viewed the morning they allowed their son to take the scenic route to school as a simple matter of consent, to their son it was the triumphant culmination of a long-running and carefully orchestrated campaign. Nigel, aged ten, was already a careful planner and effective persuader.

—⚬—

It's a commonplace observation that what you are and think and feel as a child points to a path you may take in adulthood. "The child," according to William Wordsworth, "is father of the man."[1] Teachers and parents see it all the time. The child who had a school for dolls becomes a teacher, the one who was forever constructing things an engineer. Biographical anecdotes from the lives of the famous tell the same story: JK Rowling regaled her younger sister Di with long-running, imaginative tales; by the age of seven Sir David Attenborough had his own little museum of fossils, stones and natural specimens; as soon as scientist and inventor Thomas Edison began to talk he pleaded with every adult he met to explain the workings of just about everything he encountered… to the extent that his overwhelmed teacher just couldn't take any more questions and his mother had to have him home schooled.

In the above incident we see Nigel, the future campaigner and, Nigel, the creative thinker. The consultant who invited him to revisit this memory did so under the auspices of a business organisation then called People Management International. PMI is an organisation aiming to help employees recognise their individual 'Motivated Abilities'. Its central tenet capitalises on childhood inclinations. It asserts that every individual has a unique pattern of motivation which emerges early and remains constant throughout their life. "Values and lifestyle can and do change. But your essence... does not... What you do motivationally in small measures as a child, you do largely as an adult."[2]

Nigel engaged in the SIMA (System for Identifying Motivated Abilities) process some time in the nineties and came out the other end with a personalised fifteen page document outlining those abilities and detailing where, how and to what purpose he was inclined to use them. He stashed it away amongst his papers. At one point in our final conversation he referred to this experience. He clearly appreciated the professional process which encouraged him to recognise the 'givens'. Knowing that he had been created with a range of gifts and abilities, and also limitations, was for him a source both of confidence and humility. He was comfortable in his skin. He accepted himself. And on the same basis he accepted and valued others for who they were.

One thing which stuck with him was the label attached to the role he most readily played in relation to others, ie that of a Coordinating Prime Mover.

"As a prime mover, you find it difficult to pass up the opportunity to get things started," the SIMA document states. "You relate to others as a person who initiates action and new ideas. You revel in being responsible for changes that affect a circle of people, an organisation, a community or society in general... You manage others by coordinating their performance, by bringing together their talents and energies and working along with them to accomplish a common purpose, winning their cooperation and support."[3]

Although the statement probably didn't tell him anything he couldn't have worked out for himself, Nigel appreciated the way it had been packaged and summed up in three key words: Coordinating – someone who likes to win cooperation; Prime – someone who likes to initiate things; Mover – an up and doing activist who wants to make things happen.

Parents of young children may well have come across picture books which invite their readers to find the same small character hidden somewhere on every page. The theory is that a game of spot the duck/ bear/ whatever will add value to the tale. In the same way readers of Nigel's story could be invited to spot the Coordinating Prime Mover – for these three words provide a useful summary of a pattern of behaviour we will see over and over again.

Interestingly had Nigel gone back in time to Limavady Central Primary School, his P2[4] teacher, Mrs Eileen Armstrong would have come up with a similar assessment to that of the PMI trainer. She spotted the CPM in Nigel when he was six. "He was a natural leader," she remembers. "But not in a bossy way – more by setting an example. He was a popular little boy. I knew, even then, that he would go far."

NOTES

1) William Wordsworth, from the poem 'My heart leaps up when I behold'.
2) From 'Personal Motivational Portrait of Nigel Williams', SIMA (UK) Ltd, 1993.
3) Ibid.
4) The present day equivalent of Year 2, a P(rimary) 2 class was made up of 5-6 year olds.

CHAPTER TWO

ON THE WAY TO INDIA

"Isn't it great! Dad has been promoted to Senior Valuer," Rene, positive and smiling, breaks the news to the children. "His new office will be in Portadown."

Or, to put it another way, "Pack your bags. We're moving."

I try to imagine the reactions. For Sheila it's a drama; for Sue, an adventure; for Nigel an unexpected deadline. Time is running out. By this stage his secondary education has begun and the all male world of Coleraine Academical Institution pulsates with unrealised promise – not to mention the unrealised promise that greets him each morning before he even enters its gates.

"Until I was eleven I had never really met a Catholic," Nigel would later say. "That is what can happen in a divided society." Now after eleven segregated years, when he and a handful of other Protestant boys board their school bus in Limavady, it's like wading up an exotic river of long hair, glossy lips, rippling whispers and sidelong glances. Here are banks of girls on their way to the nearby convent school. Nigel quickly discovers that a friendly "hello" is all it takes to engage with the flow of their charms. "I can tell you that all thoughts of prejudice and sectarianism disappeared as the hormones kicked in," he recalled.

In the plastic case full of his papers, I come across a school magazine entitled *CAI – December 1966*. On the opening pages are the names of all the boys who joined the school community that year, listed under the classical greeting 'salvete'. Those who left are listed under the farewell 'valete'. I picture Nigel opening it in all its fragrant freshly-printed crispness. Eagerly he looks for his name on the 'salvete' list. Yes, there it is: *Form I L A, Williams N P.* His eyes cloud over. The trouble is he'll be leaving at the end of term. That name will never feature now amongst the rugby players, rowers or athletes. If he's going to make any kind of active contribution to Coleraine Inst (and Nigel always wanted to contribute to any community he joined) he must make it fast. Suddenly the shadow lifts. There is still something he can do. Small but significant. He will volunteer to read a lesson at the Christmas carol service.

That reading would be Nigel's valete to Coleraine Inst.

Valete, Limavady.

Valete, Roe Valley Country Park.

Valete, tantalising cross-community exchanges on the bus.

—⟪⟫—

Nigel's new school, a fine, red brick state-funded co-educational grammar, stood at the top of a hill, overlooking the cream-coloured preparatory department which nestled below. Eight hundred plus pupils and forty-six staff walked, drove and cycled up the drive. Its headmaster (who pedalled daily into the carpark, a battered suitcase balanced on the bar of his bike) was the legendary Donald WJ Woodman.

When Nigel came to Portadown College, Mr Woodman, or 'the Deak' as he was affectionately known, had been headmaster for nineteen years. Nigel's year group would be the last that he would see all the way through their secondary education. Short, balding, sporting thick black glasses and an academic gown worn at half-mast over tweed jacket and baggy trousers (complete with bicycle clips), the Deak might have looked like a caretaker but his strong social conscience and belief in the value of extra curricular activities helped create a wealth of educational opportunities for his pupils. He reigned over the Portadown College like the sun – a constant source of energy and warmth.

Nigel, for his part, took full advantage of everything on offer. Over the course of the next seven years he shone on stage[1] on the athletics track[2] and on the rugby pitch, working his way up through the junior scrums to play for the Medallion and the Second XV before finally winning a coveted place, as wing forward, on the First XV.

Enter another key figure from those teenage years. Lean, totally fair, super-fit, with such a spring in his step he practically bounces into the story – it's First XV coach, Jackie Mulligan.

Jackie's entrance triggers another brief excursion into the future. Once again the youthful Nigel loses hair and gains a wife, a family, and a punishing work-schedule. The scene this time is a delightful coastal village, renowned for its golf course and its fossils. But Nigel has not retreated to Barton-on-sea to wield a golf club or a paleontologist's hammer. He's come to reflect. In this scene he is striding along the beach beneath the cliffs. (Nigel rarely walked and *never* strolled!) Around him the seagulls swoop and soar. He watches them and remembers people who have encouraged him to aim high. Over a dozen names spring to mind but topping the list is the name of Jackie Mulligan. Jackie "showed me zeal and trust in God and a disciplined lifestyle," he notes.[3]

—⁜—

Nigel's opportunity to acquire this role model began in 1971 with a cryptic announcement on the headmaster's notice-board.

'WHAT AGAIN?? – YES!!'

Those who had been part of the school community for two or more years brought newcomers up to speed. "We raise money, buy two vans, fill them with food and medicine and then a group of staff and pupils drive them all the way to India."[4]

They knew because they had done it before. In the summer of '69 a full year of fundraising had culminated in a team of four masters and five boys, led by the indefatigable Jackie Mulligan, setting off overland for Asia in two ambulances. One was delivered to Dr Victor Gardiner in West Pakistan and the second to Kachwa Christian Hospital in India. Since then Dr Gardiner had moved to a vehicle-less hospital in the Ganges Valley and Zoe Marshall, a missionary nurse stationed some one hundred miles away, had let it be known how greatly an ambulance would be appreciated in the hospital where she worked.

Fast forward eighteen months. It's 1 June 1972 – the start of the school exam season (cue for a three-week heat wave). This June, though, exams are the last thing on Nigel's mind. Today, palms sweating slightly, eyes bright with anticipation, he is watching a VW camper van with a red cross hand-painted on its side drive onto the Larne Stranraer ferry. He is a passenger in an identical van and now his van is mounting the gangway too.

The two vehicles, soon to be christened 'the Slug' and 'the Galloping Gourmet', because one is slow and the faster one carries the food supplies, have two Portadown College teachers and two students apiece on board. On the staff side Jackie Mulligan has been joined by another India trip veteran, his PE colleague Derek Wilson, along with language teacher, Paul Burrows and a mechanically-minded biologist, Alastair Uprichard. On the pupil side, Nigel's companions are three fellow rugby-players, John, Walter and Andrew. The group are on the first leg (or perhaps, in view of the distance ahead, first 'toe' would be a more appropriate term) of a journey that will take them across two continents via fourteen countries – Northern Ireland, Scotland, England, the Netherlands,

Germany, Austria, Italy, the former Yugoslavia, Greece, Turkey, Syria, Iraq, Kuwait and India – and Nigel's overriding emotion is unqualified excitement.

For the staff that excitement is more tempered. Jackie Mulligan, in particular, is conscious of the potential risks ahead. Mentally he projects forward to the extreme isolation of being thousands of miles from home, in relentless heat, with all the props removed. He knows the strain this will place on team morale and the agonised decisions that will have to be made should one of the group take sick. He's been there, done it, got the T-shirt as they say. And this time round there's the added stress of a travel deadline. On the last trip the ambulances had been driven overland to India through the Kyber Pass, but since the 1971 Indo/Pakistan conflict the Pass has closed and the team must make Kuwait by 3 July to catch a sailing across the Persian Gulf to Bombay.

Jackie is both well organised and a master of delegation. Throughout the expedition every team member has specific jobs to do. Nigel's, for example, is to keep the team supplied with chemically purified drinking water and to write up a daily log (later committed to a large scrap book and retained amongst his papers). Another member is responsible for checking tyres while someone else lights the cooker and deals with the maps. Still, no matter how meticulous the preparation, you might as well expect a commercial-free Christmas as a problem-free trip. Jackie knows the risks and declares quite openly that he is depending on God to see them through. He prays regularly about every detail. Nigel often unobtrusively joins him.

———

Next stop 23 June. The team have been driving for just over three weeks and Nigel's 'On the Road' log records huge daily mileages (day 5 – 257 miles, day 11 – 374 miles, day 15 – 276 miles) through spectacular scenery. His narrative is factually detailed, minimally reflective and uniformly upbeat in tone – a team, as opposed to a personal, diary. Problems so far have been of the trying-but-manageable variety – disruptive thunderstorms, sunburn, insect bites, sea urchin spikes, a flat tyre, petrol stations with no petrol. There are lots of observations about people and places, regular descriptions of hearty meals from tins (Chicken Walterland being a firm favourite), guitar accompanied sing-alongs and ever increasing heat. Every so often a day of 'no mileage' is recorded and the team shop, swim, write letters, play football and catch up on some sleep. This, in short, isn't *Thelma and Louise*. It's *Scouting for Boys* big time.

Of course the log doesn't tell the whole story. Off the record there has already been one major obstacle with the potential to torpedo the expedition. In Istanbul, when Jackie and Nigel had gone to the Iraqi embassy to get visas for Iraq, they had run into a wall of bureaucratic opposition. No visas. Under no circumstances would a group of British citizens be issued with visas to travel through Iraq. In his log Nigel makes a passing reference to the incident: "at the Iraqi Embassy we succeeded in getting visas only after a long wait and apparently because the consul considered Northern Ireland to be separate from the UK and not a party to British Government decisions." What he does not mention is the fact that the ambulances might have had to turn back; that he and Jackie had spent hours praying; and that the breakthrough happened seemingly by chance when a flint-faced senior official passed the pile of rejected passports towards his boss with his hand inadvertently covering the words 'United Kingdom of Great Britain' so that 'Ireland' was the word the Consul saw. "Ah, they're Irish – give them their visas," he pronounced. "A miracle" was the term Jackie used to describe this turn of events.

Now Day 23 brings further drama – again understated but intense. The group has ten days to get to Kuwait. They are currently one hundred miles from the Iraqi border and expect to cover the distance comfortably inside that time. But they have reckoned without a major hold-up at the Syrian customs (described by Nigel as "a conglomeration of vehicles, a lot of them lorries parked in higgelty-pigglety fashion"). Passports in hand, Jackie disappears into a Nissan hut. He comes out again. Even before he speaks the team can read the "brace yourselves" expression on his face.

"Well?"

"They say getting clearance will take two weeks."

Leaving the rest of the group to digest the bad news. Nigel withdraws discretely into one of the vans. A moment later Jackie joins him. Once again they are facing a major obstacle. Once again they pray that God will remove it; that the journey may go ahead as planned.

Next thing, Jackie is back inside the Nissan hut. He sets the passports down on the counter. "We're a party of eight adults and two vehicles," he smiles at the unhelpful official he had dealt with earlier. "Is there any chance you could get us through fast?"

And suddenly he's dealing with 'Mr Obliging'. The official smiles back. He places a large yet slender hand on the pile of navy blue passports and lifts his official stamp. This time there is neither rhyme nor reason for the bureaucratic change of heart. Either he is one very inconsistent individual or, as Jackie and Nigel see it, prayer has altered his response. One way or another, the crisis is over. "Contrary to expectations it only took us 1 hr to pass through customs which was nigh a miracle!! Praise God!!" Nigel records.

—ᘺ—

Four days later they're in Kuwait – making their sailing

deadline with a week to spare which is not, in fact, the bonus it might seem. Now the team have nothing to do but wait, two vans their only reliable shelter from temperatures that regularly hit 50°C. Understandably they take advantage of every bit of air conditioning they can find, passing long hours in the reading room of the British Consul. At last Monday 3 July arrives. At 3.30 pm the team drive down to the port to await their ship, the *MS Sirdhana*.

It takes a further five hours of negotiations with officialdom in the sweltering heat before they are allowed to board – and then, unexpectedly, things look up. They have boarded a ship so run down and elderly that this is its final voyage. The captain therefore determines to make it as pleasant as possible for this sticky, travel-weary party of Irishmen and bumps them up from third to first class, free of charge. So the team find themselves installed in comfortable wood-panelled cabins with port holes. They have showers, baths, dart and scrabble boards, a table tennis table (on which they compete avidly until all the table tennis balls disappear over the side of the ship), a well-stocked library, three course breakfasts, four course lunches and formal dinners at night. The ten-day voyage is smooth. "All in all, our journey aboard the *Sirdhana* has proved very relaxing, enjoyable and, gastronomically speaking, excellent!" Nigel records.

At this point he expects to leave the boat the following morning. But instead of disembarking after breakfast as anticipated, there's a delay – a delay so prolonged they must spend another night in their cabins. Intent as ever on the whinge-free reporting Nigel simply comments, "Today dragged a bit but perhaps we were keen to disembark…"

That day Jackie Mulligan has had very difficult meetings with the customs officials. He had assumed that all his meticulously completed official forms would be in order, but apparently this is not the case. "Your group can come off," is the final hard-won concession, "But the vehicles must stay on the ship."

One torturous night later, Jackie reaches for his wallet. It contains a last line of defence – not a bribe, for that would be against his principles – but a number. The friend who had slipped him this secret talisman before he left Ireland had passed it on ring-fenced with warnings to deter improper usage. "Don't phone for something bad... only something *awful.*" Now the thought of two ambulances full of medical supplies and equipment sinking to the bottom of the Indian Ocean in the hold of the stricken *Sirdhana* justifies the number's deployment.

Jackie dials and within minutes is put through to a man so well-known in Asia, that a letter addressed to 'Leybourne Callaghan, Bombay, India,' was considered over-addressed. The call is made before breakfast. "Don't worry, I'll talk to them," Mr Callaghan promises. There follows presumably a diplomatic word in certain ears and that evening Nigel is able to record:

"An eventful day starting early... We had breakfast at 9.00am, before which Mr Mulligan had contacted a Mr Callaghan, the managing director of Roche Pharmecutical Products in Bombay. (He is the brother of the Rev Sydney Callaghan in Belfast).[5] Breakfast was interrupted when we had to pass through customs so that we could land."

Thanks to Leybourne Callaghan's intervention, followed in true Good Samaritan fashion by generous hospitality, the team and the ambulances leave the ship. Still the tussle with customs continues. Eventually Walter, Andy, and two teachers set off to drive the first vehicle to its destination in Azamgarh while a third teacher, Nigel and John make the journey by train. Jackie Mulligan meanwhile sweats it out in Bombay, presenting himself at the customs office without fail every morning at 7.00 am. After a full week of this (a week, during which he makes arrangements for the rest of the group to fly home without him) he gets clearance for the second ambulance and is able to hand it over to Dr Gardiner.

The trip to India had a lasting impact. It is safe to say that there are folk in the Ganges Valley today who are able to see, or walk, or who are simply still alive thanks to the medical treatment received from the two mobile dispensaries (aka VW Camper vans) which had come all the way from Portadown.

And then there was the impact made on the team members. Nigel never forgot the smells from the bazaar in Damascus, the vision of the huge palm trees surrounding the campsite in Bagdad, the taste of the rich dark coffee they drank on the Mediterranean coast, the glorious colour of the water and the sun as they sailed across the Persian Gulf. Sights, smells, tastes, perceptions had been indelibly printed on his memory, along with a love of travel and a reflex response to every other overseas news bulletin – a phrase which would trip off his tongue so regularly that years later his wife and children would finish it for him.

"I was there," he would begin...

"On my way to India..." they would gleefully chorus.

Yet perhaps the greatest impact for Nigel lay in the experience of shared responsibility. Reading through his log, it is hard to believe that the writer was only seventeen. "Nigel seemed to arrive in the world with maturity built in," someone commented and Jackie Mulligan's tacit recognition of this certainly helped develop his pupil's leadership skills.

These were further developed by Nigel's reciprocal recognition of Jackie as a role model. Here he saw a leader who emphasised the importance of being physically fit and self-disciplined, who organised meticulously yet delegated well. He saw an encouraging, prayerful leader who knew the vital importance of team morale and balanced periods of intense exertion with times of rest. So twenty years later, during a brief time of rest at the height of gruelling political campaign, Nigel would walk along Barton beach and remember the debt of gratitude he owed to Jackie Mulligan. But he didn't leave it at that.

Most of us have a bulky mental folder labelled 'Good Intentions'. One of Nigel's distinguishing characteristics was the way he kept this aspirational folder slim – not through a lack of good intentions but through consistently carrying them out. With Nigel, perception led to action. In this case he did not simply think "I owe a lot to Mr Mulligan." He sat down a few days later and wrote his former teacher a 'thank you' note.

NOTES

1) DW Woodman loved to stage productions and Nigel loved to tread the boards. The school play in his second year was Shakespeare's *A Midsummer Night's Dream*. Nigel, impervious to jokes about his tights, gave a graceful yet menacing performance as Oberon, the Fairy King. Four years later he took on another Shakespearean role, this time as Shylock in *The Merchant of Venice* (the last PC Production that Mr Woodman would direct). "He gave an intelligent and moving presentation of one of the greatest of all parts," the producer typed on his school report that spring.

2) From 1972-73 Nigel was Athletics House Captain for Seale, one of the three School Houses, competing in the senior boys long jump, the triple jump, the 100 and 200 metre sprints, and the 400 metre and senior boys' relay races. His most notable athletic achievement had taken place a few years earlier. The moment is captured (or recreated) in a superb photograph which appeared in *The Portadown Times*. Nigel, in white shorts and singlet, is seen at full stretch in full flight, winning the intermediate boys long jump. His jump of 17ft 1in broke the previous school record by half an inch.

3) From 29 March (1989/90 journal).
4) Each team member was responsible for raising the money to cover their fare and expenses. This did not come out of the ambulance fund.
5) Rev W Sydney Callaghan was a well-known Methodist minister. He was a founder member of the NI Hospice and also of the Belfast branch of the Samaritans where he served as Deputy Director and Director for twenty-five years.

CHAPTER THREE

FRIENDS

LET'S RECOUNT A FAMILY story here. Whenever Rene wanted to embarrass her son (as every mother does from time to time) she would hark back to a long-ago Sunday morning. Nigel – aged three – sat beside her in the church pew.[1] Ten minutes into the service he started tugging at her sleeve. He needed to go to the toilet… no, he couldn't hold on… yes, he knew he'd been just before they left home… but he needed to go again… no, it couldn't wait until after the offering… he needed to go NOW. And so, with a typical maternal 'excuse-us' smile, Rene leads her small son down the aisle. Moments later, it's Nigel's turn to look apologetic. He stands in the carpark, flushed and earnest. "I didn't really need to go…" he confesses, "I was just very, *very* bored."

Somewhere between the ages of three and sixteen, Nigel's view of church changed. His Christian faith became meaningful. Indeed in his later teenage years what he believed about God and the Church and the Bible was so important to him you could not understand his life journey without taking this into account.

Nigel's final year at Portadown College was dominated by two goals – one was his desire to read Geography at Downing College Cambridge and the other was his desire to live out a radical Christian faith.

A little anecdote from his sister, Sue, gives some flavour of his general attitude at that time. She recalls her brother's response to the news (received by letter while he and the team were quietly stewing in Kuwait), that she and some friends had become Christians at a youth rally in a local church. It was like a dedicated fan hearing his team had won the FA cup. Thrilled, Nigel leapt high in the air – and fell backwards into a swimming pool.

Back home, enthusiasm undampened, his major concern was that Sue should stick with her commitment. "The things is, Susie, now you and your friends are following Jesus, you need to get into the Bible, which means," deftly he plucked Sue's *Jackie* magazine from between her fingers, "you won't want to be filling your heads with this. So here's the deal. You stop spending your pocket money on *Jackie* and put it towards buying your own Bible. And each week we'll get together with your friends for a Bible study."

The scheme worked. That autumn Sue abandoned *Jackie* and Nigel set time aside each week to instruct a bunch of impressionable fourteen-year-olds in the key biblical principles, as he understood them, of Christian discipleship.

If Nigel had been asked to summarise that understanding, he would have said something like this: You were not a Christian because you came from a Christian home, or had been baptised as a child, or attended church or tried to do the right thing. Nor could any of these things guarantee you of a place in heaven. The only thing that could do that was an experience of being put right with God through faith in Jesus Christ – a life-changing commitment which would then be fuelled by talking to God, reading the Bible, sharing with Christian friends and telling others about Jesus. In his teenage years Nigel did all these things with a passion. Sundays saw him in church. Weekdays saw him building relationships in an array of youth organisations.

There's a saying, "A friend is someone who knows the song in your heart and can sing it back to you when you have forgotten the words." That was the sort of friend Nigel aimed to be; and those were the sort of friends he found. John, Margaret, steady, humorous Norma (for a number of years Nigel's official 'girlfriend') Stephen and Claire all knew the song of faith in his heart. They came from a variety of denominational backgrounds, but they all attended both the school Scripture Union group and a Young People's Christian Endeavour group held in a church hall.

Nigel first went along to Christian Endeavour as a young teenager keen to socialise but as he and his friends matured, they developed a real hunger for spiritual growth. An acid test of any group is how they appear to a discerning outsider. The outsider in this case was a bright, articulate sixteen-year-old by the name of Derek Poole.

Derek recalls venturing into the bare wooden-floored hall, and finding a bunch of middle-class young people who were "virtually classless in their ability to include and welcome". Looking back, he recognises them as being at once "catechised in their Christian faith and understanding of the gospels" and "incredibly open to mysticism. There was a youthful zeal, but more than that you got the feeling that God was tugging at them." They were, in other words, on an adventure with God.

At this point we enter controversial waters for in the course of their spiritual adventuring, an older mentor introduced the friends to the concept of 'baptism in the Spirit'. This teaching – based mainly on the early disciples' Pentecost experience of receiving the Holy Spirit in the Upper Room[2] – was that in order to become truly effective disciples, they needed to open themselves to an infusion of spiritual power which would often manifest itself in the gift of speaking in tongues.

In much the same spiritual breath – for baptism in the Spirit was a key emphasis of the charismatic renewal at that time sweeping the Church[3] – Nigel and friends came into contact with a fledgling missionary organisation called Youth with a Misson (YWAM).[4] Some time in late 1971 or early 1972 its leaders, Lyn and Marti Green passed through Portadown (as you do) en route for Afghanistan.

The power and passion of their preaching bore out what Nigel was hearing from a Christian teacher in school. He and his friends were so taken with YWAM that in the Easter of 1972, they volunteered en masse for a YWAM missionary outreach in the Lake District. The upshot of it all was that over the next six months most of them had an experience of baptism in the Spirit. The consensus seems to be that this happened to Nigel after his return from India, some time in the August of 1972.

It would be a mistake to dismiss this incident as an emotional flash in the pan. For Nigel being filled with the Spirit was more like the installation of an inner solar panel. The dairies he kept in later life show him tapping into a constant flow of spiritual energy. From that time on he had a heightened expectancy that God could and would speak to him personally. He regularly took time out to listen – and, most significantly (in terms of this record) he chose and decided differently as a result.

Nigel's mystical immersion was followed a few months later by water baptism. One October Saturday afternoon he and a number of his friends waded out off Newcastle beach and were baptised in the chilly waters of the Irish sea. As far as they were concerned it was a straightforward act of obedience. They had read the Scriptures and seen the disciples receiving the Holy Spirit – so they had followed their example. They had also read the scriptures and seen the early disciples baptising and being baptised – so now they were doing that too.

Of course when you look at their action through the lens of Church discipline (taking account of the fact that most of the young people concerned had already been baptised as infants) it turns into an ecclesiastical and theological hot potato. Institutional considerations, however, did not weigh heavily (if at all) on Nigel's consciousness. He and his friends saw themselves as beneficiaries of a fresh, vibrant move of the Spirit, which the institutional Church was inclined to quench. "We were anabaptists before we knew it," one of them would later say. Their baptism was a statement – a statement, above all, of personal faith in Christ, but also of disaffection with a raft of 'isms' in church life (ie denominationalism, legalism, sectarianism, traditionalism) which they perceived as blocking the Spirit's power.

One reading of that Saturday afternoon on Newcastle beach is that it marked an opt-out for Nigel from the structures of institutional religion that would continue into middle-age. Later – much later – he came back into a traditional fold. But he always prized spiritual passion. "When we worship together we are celebrating in a passionate way that God has saved us all," he would preach. "Emotion is a good part of that. So I would suggest… we need to learn… the need for putting our heart and soul into our church life together. Don't get me wrong, I am in no way decrying the need for organisation, administration, planning and financial arrangements – all these are essential. But without the passion of the Holy Spirit they may be dry and empty in their outcomes."[5]

And again, perhaps it is a mistake to view Nigel's relationship with the institutional Church as a leaving and a coming back. Derek Poole regarded his friend all along as "a churchman without walls."

He saw the local church as the time and place where the sacramental life of the congregation was affirmed; "where folk encountered God, the Scriptures and each other as a means of grace," he would say. "Nigel utterly believed in the discipline of that. But he also believed that God could not be defined and contained by that reality; that the Kingdom of God was without walls in so far as God could be found unexpected places – anywhere, everywhere and with everyone."

In the light of this institutional openness, it is hardly surprising that despite his leadership skills, Nigel's adventure with God did not draw him towards the ordained ministry. Still he did not rule out other types of full-time Christian work. In the months after their water baptism, talk amongst the friends turned to university applications and future employment. Margaret wanted to do something with languages; Norma was interested in architecture; Nigel, meanwhile, had been captivated by Elizabeth Elliot's memoir [6] of her late husband Jim – a missionary, murdered along with his four colleagues in their attempt to share the Gospel with the Auca Indians of Equador. At this point Nigel saw himself in a similar pioneering role.

More immediately, though, he had to prepare for A-levels exams in Geography, Maths and Economics and Political Studies. So he plunged back into study with the same stoical determination with which a few weeks previously he had plunged into the chilly Irish sea. In the early seventies straight 'A' students were as rare as giant pandas. (Dr Andrew Dunn, a research fellow of the Institute of Independent College and University Tutors points out that whereas in 2008 "nine times more A-grades were awarded than fails… between 1965 and 1984, there were three times more fails than A-grades".[7] Yet that autumn Donald Woodman would summarise Nigel's progress with the words, "Looks like three A's on the way. A tremendous worker with outstanding ability."[8]

Some weeks later Nigel sits in the family living room, reading the newspaper.

The telephone rings and he goes out into the hall to answer it. Next moment he bursts back through the door, leaping so high in the air that his hands touch the ceiling.

"I'm into Downing," he shouts. "I've got a place."

Immediately Idwal, Sue and Sheila gather round, sharing his excitement with hugs of congratulation.

Rene is delighted too, of course. But she can't help noticing the ceiling. Its clean cream surface now makes a forensic broadcast: 'Nigel was here.' She suspects the only way to get rid of those fingerprints will be to have the whole surface repainted. Still – she smiles fondly – what harm? The smudges will act as a reminder of this very special day – and also, perhaps, as a sign that whatever he goes on to do with his life, Nigel will make his mark.

NOTES

1) Throughout their married life, Idwal and Rene remained active and committed Methodists belonging to Limavady Methodist Church and then Edenderry Memorial, Portadown. In 1990, as an active retiree, Idwal was appointed to a lay pastor's post in the historic mill town of Buckfastleigh, Devon.

2) See Acts 2: 1-4

3) 'Charismatic' is an umbrella term applied to Christians who believe that the manifestations of the Holy Spirit seen in the first century Christian Church such as miracles, prophesy and glossolalia (speaking in other tongues or languages) may still be experienced today. The word *charismatic* is derived from the Greek word χαρισμα ('gift' itself derived from χαρις. 'grace' or 'favor') which is the biblical term used describe a variety of supernatural experiences.

Rooted in the Wesleyan Holiness tradition and Pentecostalism, the Charismatic wave which Nigel encountered in the early seventies dates back to 3 April 1960. On that date 'Father' Dennis Bennet of St Marks Episcopal parish in Van Nuys California told his congregation that he had been baptised in the Spirit. He explained how this experience of a supernatural power had been accompanied by 'speaking in unknown tongues.' In the years that followed many other Christian leaders testified to a similar experience.

4) Youth with a Mission or YWAM (pronounced WYE-WAM) is an international movement of Christians from many denominations. Founded in 1960 with a primary focus of getting young people involved in short term mission work,

YWAM today involves people of all ages. The movement currently operates in 149 countries with a staff of some 16,000.

5) This is a quotation from a sermon on 1 Thessalonians 2:17- 3:5 which Nigel preached at All Saints, Peckham on 4 August 2002.

6) Elisabeth Elliot, *Shadow of the Almighty,* first published in 1958 and remains in print.

7) *The Daily Mail,* Letters, 20 August 2008.

8) Nigel achieved A grades in Geography and Mathematics and B in Economic and Political Science. On the basis of his Geography marks, he was awarded the Royal Geographical Society's prize (a £10 cheque) for the results of the Advanced Level Geography paper in the Northern Ireland General Certificate of Education (GCE) examinations for 1973.

CHAPTER FOUR

KEY QUESTIONS

NIGEL'S NEXT LEAP TOOK him from his modest family home in a provincial town, to one of the world's leading research universities. In Portadown College he had been an unassuming but impressive fish in a small stream. At Cambridge he entered the open sea, swimming in the wake of mighty giants of the deep: Sir Isaac Newton, Charles Darwin, William Pitt the Younger (not forgetting one of Downing's most notable public school alumni – the entertaining dolphin, John Cleese). Never mind the intellectual challenges, a less secure undergraduate could easily have felt the need for a cultural make-over. Yet all Nigel ditched was his school uniform, becoming significantly scruffier and hairier, striding around the gracious Downing courtyard wearing, alternately, a roll-neck shirt with a black and magenta Downing scarf, and a green and white Irish schools rugby shirt.

In terms of how he spoke, what he believed, what he did and how he went about it, Nigel saw no need to reinvent himself. You could say the Portadown College Nigel just transferred to a bigger, broader Cambridge stage. He continued to play rugby[1], took up croquet and rowing[2], attended church, involved himself in a Christian drama group (where he was once humorously described on a programme as "an Irish geographer trying to find his way home") and rose through the ranks of the Christian Union to become Vice-President of CICCU (Cambridge Inter-Collegiate Christian Union).

Essentially he did not change. At the same time, the boy from the country developed new insights and perceptions. Here was a student who had reached the age of eleven without ever rubbing shoulders with Catholics of the same age and lived his teenage years against a backdrop of sectarian murder and mayhem. One gets the impression that it was only when he arrived in Cambridge that it finally hit him what a thoroughly dysfunctional state of affairs this was.

In his first year he became friendly with a fellow geographer, Bill Adams, who had rooms nearby. "For geographers the seventies were an era of looking at first principles," Bill recalls. "We set out to explain that the world was in a mess and expound on what could be done about it. It was a do-gooding subject which appealed to Nigel's innate sense of justice." Bill has fond memories of late nights drinking coffee when they toasted crumpets on the gas fire, mused on lectures and generally set the world to rights. One lecturer, Dr Graham Chapman, taught a course on the partition of India and the ghastly consequences of the way the boundaries had been drawn. Inevitably this triggered comparisons with the partition of Ireland.

"At Cambridge I readily enjoyed the cut and thrust of college debate – mainly of the informal after-dinner kind rather than the set piece debates in the debating society," Nigel would later write. "At that time I also became increasingly concerned about Northern Ireland's political, economic and social problems. I organised prayer sessions during the time of the UWC strike[3], and constantly tried to explain the 'Northern Ireland situation' to bemused English students."[4]

Somewhere along the way he came across the Rev Jim Punton. Described as a "Youth worker and Church of Scotland minister, interested in radical theology and an enthusiast for the kingdom", everything about the man made an impact – from the passion in his voice, to the closely argued power of his words.

Essentially Punton talked about Kingdom values – and especially the value Jesus placed on compassion without strings. Jesus cared about the folk society excluded, he argued. The Church, however, tended to serve the needs of the 'haves' far more than the 'have nots' and its compassion often came with a 'dance-to-our-hymn-tune' price-tag. Punton challenged his student audience to be part of a truly alternative community, one that confronted rather than buttressed up the status quo. "Mission is about more than saving lost souls," he concluded. "Our aim should be to bring people to a real peace in Christ and address the circumstances they live in."

Punton's message raised questions for Nigel. Did he believe that the only thing you ever needed to ask about anyone was "has he/she been converted?" Did he equate the term 'social gospel' with 'losing the plot'? I picture him, chewing this over, in his late night coffee-drinking sessions, feeling rather as if he's downed a glass of lemon juice – refreshing, acerbic, subtly altering the taste of the familiar. This is the stage when it occurs to him that had he not felt called to spread the gospel in some far flung land, he might have stayed at home and become a politician. "Reaching out to people – sharing the gospel – that's the bottom line," he argues as much with himself as with anyone else. "People need Jesus – more than anything else. But we've got to be ready to get our hands dirty." In other words there are social and economic issues involved. You can't love someone in a sanitised spiritual bubble.

Back home in Northern Ireland Sheila sits in the garden writing her brother a letter. It is two weeks since Nigel set off for the summer term of his second year at Cambridge. Today the sun shines and the garden looks unusually tidy – lawn cut, borders trimmed. The very garden path has been freshly scrubbed. Tidying the garden has been Rene's project since her son left home. She misses him. They all do. Liquid-eyed Sandy has moped around the house for three days and required an egg and milk diet to sooth his upset stomach – the doggy equivalent of the letters and phone-calls that sooth everyone else.

The family all write to Nigel regularly – with Rene and Sheila his most frequent correspondents. Sheila's gentle, affectionate letters reflect a life filled with small-scale activities – baking, collecting for charity, praying with friends. She tells him all her doings – where she's been, who she's seen. Once in a while she refers to her part-time job in an old people's home and very occasionally she hints at the depressive illness that began in her teenage years and continues to limit her. This year, though, has been better and today her mind is very definitely taken up with other things.

"I expect you heard on the news about the man who was shot dead near our church," she begins. "Dad was out with the dog late on Friday night when it happened. Susie and I heard the shots in bed and Susie was nearly up the walls because she thought someone had shot Dad."[5]

Rene also refers to the shooting in her letter.[6] "As far as we know there was a sectarian motive…" she observes. The striking thing here is the 'that-explains-it' tone – a reminder that, as one commentator put it, "From the beginning of the modern troubles in Northern Ireland in the late 1960's until the end of the twentith century, a citizen of Northern Ireland was over 200 times more likely to die from sectarian violence than a citizen of India."[7] Sectarian riots, bombings and shootings had become the grim back-drop against which everyone lived out their daily lives. As far as Rene was concerned this incident was notable simply because it happened so close to her own front door.

One reference and she moves on to happier things, namely the finals of a missionary quiz, her fund-raising sponsored slim, and the cakes she has posted so that Nigel will have a taste of Northern Irish home-baking to share with his Cambridge friends. Then, putting her pen and letter into her apron pocket, she steps out of the sunlit garden and into her cluttered kitchen to cut sandwiches for tea. Rene is not given to introspection. Still, she reflects that it won't be so very long until Nigel returns for the summer – or part of it, anyway. And she resolves to send him more cakes if she can. For next year he'll be finished at Cambridge – and after that, well, who knows? Who knows where he will go, or what he will do then?

Summer 1975 saw Nigel on the hippy trail – one of fifteen young people off for a month-long missionary outreach in Morocco. His vivacious school-friend Margaret, a second year language student at Queen's University, was part of the same group. For the last two years she and Nigel had been a couple. Still, the trip did not mean romantic strolls along sun-baked paths. YWAM were as down as the tazman on any hint of duality of purpose. When the young folk divided into two teams, Margaret went with one and Nigel with the other.

Of course this was a miniscule sacrifice compared to the sacrifices Nigel saw up ahead. Over the last few years he had continued to devour missionary biographies – Hudson Taylor, Brother Andrew, Jim Elliot. The achievements of these heros of the faith inspired him. Here were people who had made a real difference in the world, risking everything to share God's word – with Elliot dying in the attempt. His maxim, "he is no fool who gives up that which he cannot keep to gain that which he cannot lose" was one with which Nigel always identified and often quoted. He too had steeled himself to follow Christ to the outermost reaches of the global village – the densest African jungle, the remotest Himalayan settlement. Name your spot, he was ready to serve Christ there. Yes, even if it killed him.

Nigel imagined his Moroccan trip would nourish this ambition. He went looking for prophetic words and burning bushes. What he got was a test of his powers of endurance. Soon after crossing into Africa he picked up a stomach bug. It made him constantly sick and the staple diet of vegetable curry didn't help.

This, then, was the context in which his path crossed that of a sinewy spiritual warrior who had been serving God in Morocco for twenty years. Normally buoyant and full of energy, Nigel for once was drained. Yet his desire to give his all had not wavered. "When I finish college, I'm thinking of working with YWAM or some other agency," he confided. Probably he hoped for affirmation, advice, encouragement. At the very least some mild expression of pleasure would have been nice. Instead this role model gave him a long, level look.

"You grew up in Northern Ireland – a place where religion has been so tarnished. Why are you not thinking of going back and living a true Christian life in a divided society?"

Nigel had been floored. He hadn't known how to reply. On the journey home, even with Margaret by his side, expressing concern over the amount of weight he'd lost and enthusing at the prospect of further YWAM trips, he simply could not get what the man had said, nor the way he'd said it, out of his head.

━━ ⁂ ━━

One Tuesday, not long after Nigel's return to Downing, Rene, Idwal and Sheila all wrote on the same day. Gentle Sheila shared a reading from Psalm 91. She assured her brother that "all the Lord wants us to do is dwell in the secret place of the most High... under the shadow of his wings"; busy Rene was glad to hear that "the blazer and cake arrived OK" and wrote of the dizzying number of voluntary organisations that she had worked with that week; informative Idwal enclosed an obituary from the Monday edition of the *Belfast Telegraph* – an obituary for DW Woodman. "I am going to the funeral service in St Mark's tomorrow so you will be remembered," he noted. "Because so many of the staff wish to go, and as a mark of respect, PC is closing at lunchtime tomorrow."[8]

No doubt Nigel experienced a mixture of emotions as he read his post, strongest of which may well have been the sense of the end of a chapter. On leaving Portadown College, he had written to his headmaster and received a typically warm reply. Mr Woodman had hoped that their relationship would continue "on a non-professional basis: just friendship." That special link with his schooldays had now gone.

Chapters, in both the literal and metaphorical sense, continued to dominate Nigel's thinking that autumn. On the one hand were all the questions surrounding the next chapter in his own life journey. And on the other, the physical chapters of the dissertation he was writing on a subject close to his questioning heart: *An Historical Study of Religious Segregation in Tanderagee, Northern Ireland.*

Lest the citizens of Tanderagee (or Tandragee, as it is more commonly known), feel unfairly maligned, let it be clearly stated that today this rural plantation town is a tranquil place, famous for its potato crisps. In his introduction Nigel acknowledges as much. "Relationships between the two communities in the town in present times are very good, and it has experienced very little violence," he states. The fact is he could just as easily have studied religious segregation in any plantation town but this one offered him good source material for the task.

Nigel's original aim was to examine the changing pattern of spatial separation between the Catholic and Protestant communities who lived there over the centuries. Before long, though, he modified this plan. In the first section of his dissertation he broadens it out into a general overview of writings on 'the Troubles'. Here we find scholarly definitions, studies of the way fear and mistrust had driven Catholics and Protestants apart, a portrait of two communities expressing group identities in defence (raise the barricades), avoidance (live separate lives) and attack (shoot, bomb and riot).

Then in the second section he narrows his focus down to concentrate not on Tanderagee through the ages, but solely on that town's seventeenth century past. With academic objectivity, he charts the confiscation of lands from the rebellious O'Hanlon clan who were showing the natural resistance of a native population – an apparent attempt to rid the area of O'Hanlons to thwart future uprisings.

"Sir Oighe's son and heir was sent to Sweden… His wife had recently given birth to a baby, and she was dragged off to the woods by soldiers in the government service, and was stripped and left there to die the next day."

The disturbing seventeenth century account continues as Nigel records the granting of the lands to a distinguished soldier, Sir Oliver St John; the growth of a prosperous little town (amongst the thirty-five listed as the backbone of the Plantation); the uneasy relationships between British settlers and native Irish culminating in the rebellion of 1641. For a brief period Patrick Oge O'Hanlon gets his own back, capturing Tanderagee church and castle and making prisoners of the English and Scottish settlers. Then, once more, the tables turn. The rebellion is put down; the church and castle are rebuilt – but not before the prisoners, women and children included, have been herded to the water-side, "stripped naked, knocked on the head, and thrown into the river."

There's a saying that to get a real grasp of any subject you need to consider three things: the history, the questions and the answers. Nigel's dissertation gave him his first real opportunity to delve into the history of 'the Troubles'. His research developed his social understanding in much the same way as Punton's preaching had broadened his theology. Phrases from the historical records ('dragged off', 'stripped naked', 'left to die') could so easily have been taken from a contemporary news bulletin. By the time he had finished he had recognised a vicious pattern of resentment, fear and brutality wheeling across the centuries into a present where tit for tat atrocities were murderously common. "It would be an over-simplification to say that the root of all conflict between the communities in Northern Ireland can be traced to 1608, but no doubt many of the *trends* for future relationships began at that time," he concludes.

Another student might have left it at that. But Nigel could not put down his pen without scratching around for some answers. This study had caused him much heart-searching. One thing that had particularly struck him was the gap between individual experience and group attitudes. Catholics and Protestants often had a warm relationship on a one-to-one basis but that warmth did not extend to their perception of the group as a whole.

So he finishes with a recipe for progress. Individuals should "face up to the challenge of carrying though their personal friendliness towards individuals of the 'other side' into their political identity and actions as a member of their own group," finding hope in the biblical promise that love will cast out fear.

Glib words from a youthful idealist, one might say – but remember, with Nigel, action always followed closely on the heels of thought.

NOTES

1) He played for Downing 2nd XV in his second year, having chosen not to play in his first year in order to give more time to Christian drama.

2) He rowed in the summer of each year – 6th, 5th and 3rd boats respectively.

3) The Ulster Workers Council (UWC) Strike was a general strike lasting two weeks from 15–28 May 1974. It was called in protest against the proposals in the Sunningdale Agreement to provide sharing of political power between unionists and nationalists and a role for the government of the Republic of Ireland in the governance of Northern Ireland. It succeeded in bringing down the power-sharing Northern Ireland Executive whereupon responsibility for the government of Northern Ireland reverted to Westminster under the arrangements for Direct Rule.

4) From 'A Political Career?', 27 July 1983.

5) Letter dated 27 April 1975.

6) Letter dated Sunday 28 April 1975.

7) Tony Wright, *British Politics – A Very Short Introduction*, Oxford University Press, 2003, p4.

8) Letters dated 28 October 1975.

CHAPTER FIVE

MARCHING TO A
DIFFERENT DRUM

AMONGST THE LETTERS NIGEL saved in a small red file there is one from his father dated 6 Nov 1975. "My dear Nigel," it begins, "The address you require is: Civil Service Commission, Rosepark House, Upper Newtownards Road, Belfast... I'm told there is a pruning exercise going on to reduce expenditure on staff and that proposals for entry in 1976 have not been finalised! No harm in writing... to see what result you get."

Nigel did write – and his communication paid off. With the ink scarcely dry on his geography degree, he moved home to work in the civil service as a graduate administration trainee. Bill Adams, who had not seen much of him in his final year, felt a surprise akin to that of watching someone walk determinedly down an up escalator – an escalator, in this case, designed to carry young people out of Northern Ireland. It wasn't even as if his decision could be explained by a romantic attachment, as by then, Nigel's relationship with Margaret had reverted back to one of warm friendship. Bill recalled that Nigel had been given to making unexpected decisions, and simply concluded that he marched to a different drum.

"Returning to Northern Ireland in 1976 to take up my job as a Civil Servant was a crucial decision and one that I believe God spoke to me clearly about," Nigel would later write. "I was very taken with the story of Daniel who studied for three years (as I had done at Cambridge) and then entered government service;

and also the stories of Nehemiah and Joseph who were the rough equivalent of senior civil servants. Furthermore, whereas previously I had envisaged that a natural progression from Cambridge might lead me to Christian service abroad of some kind (the Christian Union at Cambridge of which I was Vice-President, was very missionary orientated), it was a Moroccan missionary who encouraged me to see Northern Ireland as a mission field 'crying out for spiritual leaders'."[1] In other words he deliberately returned to Northern Ireland to face up to the challenge of Christian living on his own home patch.

Nigel came home in 1976 – a year which began with a bloodbath. In early January two Catholics were murdered at their South Armagh farmhouse, then three Catholic men were gunned down by loyalists in Co Down, followed by ten Protestant workers murdered by the IRA in South Armagh as they came home from work in a minibus. Briefly the Province seemed to teeter on the brink of civil war and then, amid calls for calm, it steadied again. Grim-faced, people went about their business. The wheels of Direct Rule continued to turn.

For one newly-fledged civil servant this meant a daily commute from his parents' home in Portadown to the Department of Commerce in Chichester House, Belfast. There Nigel shared a functional office with another administrative trainee, Ivor Greer. "We became good buddies," Ivor recalls. "As staff officers we often wrote drafts of speeches for ministers. We used to vie with each other to see how much of what we wrote would make it through to the final draft unchanged." The wordsmith in Nigel relished this challenge and the opportunity it provided to hone and sharpen his policy writing skills. Another colleague from that time remarked on his kindness, intellectual brilliance and, intriguingly, on his "propensity to sit cross-legged on the top of filing cabinets while working".

Outside work Nigel looked for ways to build bridges in a divided society. Initially he felt drawn to drama. That winter he set about recruiting a Christian drama group – the Kallah players. He then proceeded to script, direct and act in a drama based on Calvin Miller's inspirational allegory, 'the Singer' (giving a typically memorable performance as the devil).

In the taut, depressed, bomb-blasted city that was Belfast in the 1970s, a vibrant cultural night-life seemed as far-removed as the Niagara Falls. Even going to the pub was risky. Still, people, in very respectable numbers, braved deserted streets to come and see Nigel's play. They liked what they saw. Any other impresario would surely have been encouraged to repeat this success. But Nigel sensed a cul-de-sac. Strategically he had gone as far as he could go along this particular route; so he stepped back from the Kallah players. The way ahead, he recognised lay in co-operating with a group of like-minded Christians. The question now became which group?

—m—

The setting is a high-ceilinged front room in a large detached house (No 83) off a broad leafy suburban thoroughfare (Belfast's Ravenhill Road). It's Sunday morning and this room is packed. Thirty young adults and around a dozen children have gathered together. They are singing. Lifting their hands. Praising God. Nigel is there too – there at the invitation of the leader – there, to a certain extent, on spec.

The worship time ends, but no-one hurries away. This is a fellowship characterised, as one member put it, "by a strong sense of family coupled with a sense of liberty and freedom from the traditional rules of Northern Ireland." The whole ethos promotes supportive friendships and social networking. Children play. Adults chat. Some of the chats are intense and lead to further prayer. There is no dividing wall between the spiritual and the social…

Nigel has come looking for a body of like-minded believers that will help him in his quest to reach out across the sectarian divide. It could be said, with some justification that, at the time, such churches were as thin on the ground as the hairs on a bald man's scalp. In fairness it should also be said that throughout the history of the Troubles there were always leaders from both traditions ready to walk the path of reconciliation with vision and courage and there were ordinary people ready to follow them. Did the Ravenhill Park Fellowship fall into this category? The group had formed under the umbrella of the charismatic renewal[2] – a stream of church life which had brought Christians from different traditions together. Its leader, David Matthews, had a warm brotherly relationship with Des Dick the leader of a Catholic community in Andersonstown and there were plans for the two groups to share activities from time to time.

Nigel decides to commit himself to the group – and, never one to do things by halves, to move into the area. So in 1977 he becomes the proud owner of a batchelor pad. The property is two up, two down, with an outside loo and he pays less for it than you'd pay today for a settee and a couple of armchairs.

—∿∿—

Now for a love story. One Saturday morning Nigel sits drinking coffee in the home of fellowship members, Ronnie and Margaret Wilson, when another member drops by. He already knows Heather Ross by sight. She is one of the three single women who have recently moved into 83 Ravenhill Park when David Matthews and his family moved out. This is the first time they had ever really talked, though – the first time he has properly noticed her poise, good sense, warm humour and the way she can light the whole room up with a smile. All of a sudden he knows he wants to see her again – soon! "I've just moved into 50 O'Meath Street," he tells her. "Why don't you call round?"

Less than forty-eight hours later his doorbell rings. He glances out of the window. Yeees! Heather's yellow mini is parked out on the street and, better still, Heather herself is on the doorstep. The very fact that she hasn't wasted any time before coming confirms him in the opinion that here truly is a girl after his own heart. "Come in, come in." Eagerly he leads her into the kitchen come living-room with its brand new table. Just as he hopes, the conversation flows until a visit from another member of the fellowship puts paid to their tête a tête. Such is the downside of being part of a sociable group – George doesn't go home until midnight!

When Heather next sits at the pine table two weeks later, her host ensures there will be no such interruptions. He serves her pork chops in tomato sauce and then suggests they drive to a local beauty spot on the shores of Belfast Lough for a walk along the beach. Again Heather's response is everything he could hope for and more. She simply presses her car keys into his hand, which, considering that her mini has cost more than his house, is a considerable expression of trust.

By the end of that walk it is very clear to any passers-by that the tall dark-haired young man and the slim girl at his side are a couple. Nigel is in love with Heather and he woos her (not that she needs much wooing) with a disarming openness.

"Heather there are three things you need to know about me," he tells her that afternoon. "One – I wear glasses. Two – I'm likely to be bald by the time I'm thirty. And three – I've false teeth." He also talks to her about the future, about his interest in politics and his feeling that he might be called to some future political role.

No doubt, even as he makes a clean breast of both shortcomings and ambitions, he knows he is on safe ground. The bond which has developed so rapidly between them is much stronger than the prospect of fading good looks. They announce their engagement in a matter of weeks.

—⁂—

Shortly before that announcement Nigel and his mum had an interesting little conversation. Rene and Idwal could see early on where their son's relationship with Heather was headed, and much as they liked the young teacher from South Armagh, they had a question or two.

"If you and Heather were getting married in a church in Belfast, what church would it be?" Rene asked.

Nigel shrugged, "I don't know. We haven't discussed it."

"Well, if Heather was getting married at home in Armagh, what church would it be?" Rene persisted.

This question too drew a blank. Nigel was not being deliberately obtuse, he just didn't understand what his mother really wanted to know... so she was forced to dispense with diplomacy and ask straight out:

"Nigel, is Heather a Catholic or a Protestant?"

That Rene felt she needed to ask this question about someone Nigel had met at church was indicative of the unconventional nature of the Ravenhill Park Fellowship.

—⁂—

December arrived and while the rest of the population sang carols, wrapped presents and shopped, Nigel and Heather got married. Most people don't pledge their troth on a Thursday four days before Christmas, but theirs was a wedding with a difference.

It had many traditional elements: a beautiful bride in ivory given away by an elder brother (her parents having died some years before); three bridesmaids in apple green; a groom and the best man looking dashing in dark green velvet jackets, bow ties and frilled dress shirts; a typical congregation of family and friends. The difference somehow came through in a sense of community ownership. This was a house church wedding. The legal formalities had already been completed in the registry office beforehand. David Matthews conducted the ceremony, other members of the fellowship sang. Janet Preston, the wife of another elder, danced down the aisle before the happy couple, who had written their own vows. The meal afterwards was provided by the women in the group. All in all the whole event unfolded with a distinctive blend of spiritual fervour, informality and fun. Maybe here and there amongst outsiders to the fellowship an eyebrow was raised, but the joy was infectious and everyone had a great time!

Hold onto the thought of those raised eyebrows. The next episode in Nigel's story comes with a warning. It doesn't contain flash photography, bad language or violence – but those of a conservative fundamentalist disposition may find what follows disturbing.

For a start, there is the underlying assumption (commonly held by those who had embraced the charismatic experience) that when Christians gather together in worship, God may choose to speak directly into their particular circumstances through the gift of 'prophecy'. What this means is that certain people will pass on verbal and/or visual messages to others (sometimes to individual believers, sometimes to the whole group). Where verbal, the messages will often be given in tongues and then interpreted.

A further challenging (for some) assumption is that those from Catholic backgrounds who are filled with the Spirit of Christ and remain within the Catholic Church, are truly 'saved' in the Protestant evangelical understanding of the word. And equally that Spirit-filled people from Protestant backgrounds who love and follow Jesus, yet do not recognise the authority of Rome, are fully-fledged members of the mystical Body of Christ and Church of God.

These were two of the spiritual givens which Nigel carried with him when, five months after his wedding, he set off for a weekend leadership conference in the Christian Renewal Centre in Rostrevor.

"See you on Sunday," he kissed Heather goodbye and away he went – off to the gracious conference centre on the water-lapped shores of Carlingford Lough.

Some of the men arriving at the Renewal Centre that Friday like Nigel, had driven from East Belfast, others had come from West Belfast. Some were Protestant. Others were Catholic. Their coming together was the latest development in an ongoing relationship between Ravenhill Park Fellowship and Andersonstown Community – a relationship pioneered by David Matthews and David Preston (another Ravenhill Park Fellowship elder) on one side and Des Dick, on the other.

None of these leaders had foreseen what was to happen during the first worship session on Saturday morning. Nigel went into it expecting spiritual refreshment along with some new insights on leadership. Chatting to the other men beforehand he found them in much the same frame of mind. And then they started to pray. The spiritual temperature rose. Suddenly there was a prophesy about unity... about God's desire for Ravenhill Park Christian Fellowship and Andersonstown Community to become one. It was followed by another and another... The atmosphere was electric. Participants could scarcely take in what they were hearing. They were stunned.

Nigel returned on Sunday shocked... amazed... awed.

"We're going to unite with Andersonstown," he told Heather. "It wasn't our idea. God spoke. We spent the rest of the weekend trying to work how to go about it."

–––∞–––

Despite the obstacles, within a matter of months both Ravenhill Park Fellowship and Andersonstown Community died and a new entity, Belfast Christian Family, was born.[3] Whilst some members struggled with the new developments, Nigel revelled in them. Was this not an opportunity to do the very thing he has envisaged in his dissertation – an opportunity to build group relationships across the religious divide? He delighted in the challenge to make things work practically and realise high ideals in the nitty gritty of daily life.

"It's easy to desire unity, to sing about it, and to have a large conference with hundreds of Protestants and Catholics." Des Dick said afterwards. "But to build a community where Protestants and Catholics start sharing their lives, opening up their homes, their marriages, their finances to each other, to deal with suspicion and hostility, that's taking it further. It isn't good enough just to have weekends together or go to conferences. We need to build community. It costs a lot and it seems that not many are prepared to pay. It's simpler to stay in your own patch of land and wave at people in the other field."[4]

Simpler indeed – as Nigel discovered when he took on the task of producing a 'family' news sheet. This functional A4 page publication, called *Hap'nings*, aimed to inform the whole group, now meeting in the Minor Hall of the YMCA in Belfast City Centre on Tuesday evenings, of events in the weeks ahead. The first issue clearly missed the mark. To Nigel's dismay, the Catholic members of the group largely left their copies of *Hap'nings* behind.

He raised the matter with the men who had been together in Rostrevor at their next prayer-time. "They had difficulty with your opening sentence," he was informed. What! Nigel had invested time and thought in that sentence – and come up with something suitably innocuous. How could anyone possibly take issue with the innocent words, "This is the first edition of our church newsletter"?

"The problem is the word 'church'", Des explained. "It means different things to Catholics and Protestants. To your East Belfast folk it simply implies 'a local community of believers'; but to the West Belfast folk there's only one church in the proper sense, the Roman Catholic Church. Any other use of the word implies a separation from this church. They didn't take *Hap'nings* home because they couldn't risk it being seen and misunderstood."

Let's look again at Des's statement. In his explanation one word really deserves to appear in neon lights – the word 'risk'. Belfast Christian Family had come into being at a time when people were targeted for the company they kept. Stray Catholics in Protestant areas could be shot and vice versa – a brutal generalisation pointing up the courage the whole enterprise required – especially on the part of the leaders. These folk challenged a fear-fuelled status quo. While the barricades went up and the bombs went off around them, they marched to a different drum. Briefly but honourably they incarnated an expression of oneness between Protestants and Catholics based on the belief that loving Jesus was the single vital requirement for unity.

In this spirit, Nigel took the set-back with *Hap'nings* on the chin. He truly wanted to develop understanding. He listened and he learnt, and others learnt too. Little by little the barriers between people came down. Honestly they discussed their separate identities. They did not even shirk (as will be seen in the next chapter) from tracing fractured relations back to their seventeenth century roots.

NOTES

1) From 'A Political Career?', 27 July 1983.

2) See Chapter Three Note 3. The charismatic movement created a new openness to the range of spiritual gifts listed in 1 Corinthians 12: 8-10 in the mainline denominations but it also provoked considerable opposition. As a result many 'charismatic' leaders left traditional churches and started independent fellowships.

3) In terms of how they related to the institutional church, members from the Ravenhill Park Fellowship side of Belfast Christian Family remained an independent fellowship whilst members from Anderstown Community remained within the Roman Catholic Church.

4) 'I'm alright, you're alright', interview with David Preston and Des Dick, *Streams* magazine.

CHAPTER SIX

GOLDEN AGE

As A GROOM-TO-BE, Nigel had spent the ten weeks leading up to his marriage commuting from Belfast to London for a work-related course. The first Friday evening, when Heather picked him up from the airport, their reunion was everything she could have hoped for. Not so his Sunday evening departure. Romeo kissed his Juliet goodbye, grabbed his hand luggage from the trolley and charged off down the corridor without a backward glance. Deprived of what she considered an essential part of a loving farewell, Heather watched him stride off into the departure lounge, nursing a sense of hurt. "I had to train him to turn round and wave," she said later. "He was always moving on to the next thing. But he learnt to look back, because he understood what it meant to me."

At one level this little anecdote has an apocryphal 'Men-are-from-Mars-Women-from-Venus' ring to it. At another it illustrates an important quality in Nigel and Heather's relationship. Though naturally dominant and given to forging on ahead, Nigel always made space to listen to Heather's views. They talked things through. "You think you love each other now, but your love will grow as they years go by," David Matthews had said on their wedding day and he never spoke a truer word.

Before long there was a numerical as well as a qualitative growth in the Williams home. A first daughter, Kathryn came into the world on 1 December 1979. A son, Simon, arrived under two years later, closely followed by a second daughter, Lynda in early 1983 and finally Elizabeth in 1985. At one stage, therefore, there were four children under the age of six in the Williams' home.

Amongst many other things this meant a huge expenditure on nappies and none whatsoever on alarm clocks. Still Nigel saw to it that the word 'lie-in' did not become for Heather the equivalent to 'feast' to a starving man. On Saturday mornings while he made breakfast, she gloried in a precious half-hour snooze. Now any mother of four would give the man in her life a medal for simply corralling their offspring into the kitchen and ending up with more cereal in them than on them. But Nigel didn't do 'functional' – especially where his family were concerned. He turned the kitchen table into an art gallery. To this day Kathryn, Simon, Lynda and Elizabeth all fondly remember the excitement of waiting to be called down to the kitchen where they would each find their breakfast arranged as a food-picture – smiley orange and grape faces, toast sail windmills and chocolate bottomed boats.

On the domestic front these years bear all the hallmarks of a golden age – a season marked by Nigel and Heather's love for one another and by the closeness of their relationships with others.

The blossoming of these wider relationships came – as major Williams developments tended to do – with a change of address. At a first glance you wouldn't have noticed anything especially idyllic about Nigel and Heather's new home – an unpretentious three-bed semi in pleasant Ladas Drive. The significant thing was that they shared a driveway with David and Janet Preston, also members of Belfast Christian Family. More significant still: before long a gate in the back garden led the Williams into the adjoining gardens of three other community families. That meant five families with, by 1985, seventeen children between them all living within a stone's throw of each other. The group had deliberately opted for this physical expression of 'community' (known as a 'cluster') to give one another practical and spiritual support and to make a positive difference in their neighbourhood. The fact that, years later, all five families would look back on this period with the sense of something precious which they had once known but were never able to recapture, is a measure of the cluster's success.

Piecing together anecdotal accounts of this period gives a picture of a typical gathering. It's 8.00 pm and the couples are coming together for their weekly meeting in the Preston's long lounge. Gary and Alice and Roy and Kate arrive first. Nigel and Heather come in on their heels. While the women catch up on the latest community news, Nigel arranges to borrow a lawn mower from practical Gary, and David and Roy swap stories from the world of education. "Hi there!" Philip bursts into the room, followed a few moments later by Sadie who drops a pot of home-made jam into the kitchen en route for the lounge. The next few moments are spent sorting out the long white flexes of the baby monitors which snake across the floor and out of doors and windows connecting each set of parents to their sleeping offspring.

With each member of 'the cluster' present and the practical arrangements in place, David introduces the topic for that evening. They have already discussed all sorts of matters – TV, children's books and comics, school, pocket money, discipline – aiming to agree on a consistent approach in each area. Tonight David suggests that they focus their thoughts on that perennial parental bugbear 'peer pressure'. Nigel nods thoughtfully, but before he can make an opening contribution, the monitor at Heather's elbow emits a ringing sound – faint but clear.

At this Nigel leaps to his feet. "Telephone! Sorry." He hurries out of the room, only to return a few minutes later. "That was quick," says Roy. Nigel shrugs. "It stopped ringing just as I got through the door."

And then, before he can sit down, the faint ringing recurs. Again Nigel bounds from the room. And again he's back a few moments later to report a second missed call.

The third time, when the phone rings, everyone laughs. "Leave it." Gary urges. But they all know that Nigel won't. Communication is his life-blood. He could never lean back in an armchair, knowing someone was trying to get in touch with him and not knowing who it was or what it was about. This time he literally shoots from his seat, determined to reach the elusive caller before they give up. Only, of course, once again the phone stops ringing just as he opens his front door – because the whole thing is a set up – an elaborate practical joke, fondly orchestrated by Nigel's electronically minded cluster colleagues.

This combination of fun, warm friendship and intimate fellowship made life in Ladas Drive wonderfully enriching. Occasionally the five families ate together. During the week they shared babysitting and child-care arrangements. The children meanwhile grew up with a strong sense of an extended family – moving in and out of five homes (and gardens) where everyone followed rules based on the same values.

It has to be said that not everyone involved in the wider 'House Church' movement had such a positive experience. Some folk emerged hurt and spiritually confused – particularly by the system of pastoral authority known as 'shepherding'[1]. By and large, though, Belfast Christian Family avoided authoritarian extremes. As far as Nigel was concerned, he was always careful to consult with the leadership before taking any major decisions, but when, at one point, a 'Shepherd' attempted to put brakes on his whistle-stop courtship of Heather, he pointedly turned a deaf ear. Though totally committed to a shared life-style, Nigel remained his own man.

"This morning I thank God for a good family life," he wrote

during this era. "For the joys of Sunday together. The meeting, having the Prestons to coffee (the kids played so happily) a lovely lunch, a game together, Matthew Dick's christening, bed. I suppose underlying it is a very sound relationship with Heather which blesses me enormously."[2]

Quality relationships. Those are the defining words. In addition to the cluster group meetings, Nigel met on a regular basis with other members of the leadership team and was responsible himself for leading a 'sharing' group of half-a dozen men. To some a 'sharing group' for men might seem a contradiction in terms – but for Nigel having a group of 'brothers' that he could talk to and pray with added enormously to his well-being. "What's most on your mind at the moment? What is your greatest inner difficulty? What's been your closest moment to God? What is God teaching you?" He thrived on responding to such questions and on the spiritual discernment and practical advice which these friends could give.

---※---

By spring 1982 Nigel had been back in Northern Ireland for five and a half years. In that period he had married, fathered two of his four children, moved three times (each move to a slightly bigger house), assumed leadership responsibilities in his church community and been recently promoted to work in the Industrial Development Board (where he was the youngest person ever at his particular civil service grade).

He had also written a series of articles for the *Belfast Telegraph* detailing routes to places of interest throughout Northern Ireland. His 'Off-the-Beaten-Track' columns guided readers to the Province's gentle dolmens, enchanting inlets, gracious loughs, hidden villages and famous apple orchards. They proved so popular, Nigel received the recognition of a British Airways

Tourism Endeavour Award. "No home visitor or holiday maker should have been without (the series) this summer," was the adjudicators' verdict.[3]

It is sadly ironic to note how often the newspaper page on which 'Off the Beaten Track' appeared contained a jarring counterpoint in the form of a report or comment on the latest sectarian death. For 1981, the year when Nigel began his columns, was the year of the Republican hunger strikes. It saw the unionist MP and Methodist Minister, Rev Robert Bradford gunned down, along with the caretaker, in the community centre where he was holding his clinic. It also saw Belfast Christian Family produce a significant folder of leaflets entitled 'Sins of the Fathers'.

One aim of this well-produced little document, to which Nigel contributed under the pen name Bill Prichard, was to set out how Belfast Christian Family continued to address the issues faced by ordinary people from different cultural backgrounds seeking to worship and serve God together. It attracted a certain amount of publicity on publication. But its main importance lay as much in the fact that it happened as in what it said.

The 100-strong membership of Belfast Christian Family reflected the religious breakdown of the wider population at that time – one third was Roman Catholic and two thirds Protestant. In 'Sins of the Fathers' they displayed an honest, pragmatic approach to historical and doctrinal differences[4] and gave expression to political and spiritual aspirations in a manner which both Catholic and Protestant members of the group could accept. As David Matthews put it at the start of the closing paragraph, "The fact that we of Belfast Christian Family... sat down together to produce this profile is some small glimmer of hope".[5] More than a quarter of a century later, it is easy to forget that those words were written at a time when hope was in very short supply.

Notwithstanding so much progress, Nigel had questions. Yes, his life was undoubtedly rich, undoubtedly fulfilling but he could not ignore the huge social and spiritual needs all around him. He did not want to become complacent. He longed to do more.

First thing each morning he habitually took time to pray and read the Scriptures. On one such morning, as he prayed, Nigel had an experience which would mark the course of the next two decades. Indeed, in the great hall of memory, out of all the key scenes clamouring for recognition, this one deserves a place at the top table.

That morning Nigel sensed God speaking to him. In the years that followed he came back to the words that had impressed themselves on him again and again. This is part of what he noted in his journal.[6]

> *Listen to my vision*
> *Listen to what I have for you*
> *It is something really good*
>
> *Don't opt out of Church*
> *Don't close off the source of life*
> *For your God will bless you still…*
>
> *Still you must prepare*
> *Still you must learn from me*
> *Until you are ready.*
>
> *Ready for what O Lord?*
> *Ready to do what?*
> *Ready to give myself for you.*

You will be sent out
To help change this country
To bring my words of life…

You will have to work for it
It will not come easily
And you'll need your family.

Activate politically
See what I will say to you
See what changes I will bring
See what changes I will bring.

'Activate politically' – that was the phrase that resonated with him most strongly. Here, he sensed, was the 'more' that he hungered for. The notion of a political career had been there, lurking in the bushes, throughout his student days. Now it crashed out of the foliage to become his heart's desire… his lode star… his dream. More than that – it was the dream he felt that God had planted in him.

There are those, such as the proselytising atheist Richard Dawkins, who are utterly scathing of anyone who believes in revealed truth. "Deluded and dangerous" was the verdict I once heard him pass on an academic professor who made it clear that he held an a priori faith position. I found myself thinking of Nigel. What would Dawkins have made of the diaries I'd been reading? What, indeed, would he have made of this 'prophetic word'? Doubtless he would have been more scathing than ever of a man who not only believed in God, but believed this God spoke in such a direct and personal way. Was it delusion – to be explained away in psychological or neurological terms? All Nigel would have asked was that the reader might receive his story and consider it with an open mind.

For his own part, in the aftermath of the experience, Nigel went and talked things over with David Preston – explained what had happened and showed him the message. He had spent the last few hours trying to get his head round it. Clearly, if God was calling him to exert an influence in the political sphere, it would mean huge changes. "I'll have to leave the civil service, find some other means of support, get myself a constituency…"

As the words poured out, his friend assessed what he heard. A level-headed spiritual leader at a time when emotional excess was all too common, David recalls responding with cautious encouragement. He felt somewhat unsure what prophetic weight should be placed on the message but confirmed its sense that God would extend Nigel's influence. He remained supportive. He also helped Nigel make the transition from the spiritual heights to the mundane realities of nappies and office deadlines.

By the time they parted company, the chat had turned to other things – the next cluster meeting, the forthcoming edition of *Hap'nings*. Nigel had settled back into routine. To an extent it was as if the events of that morning had been overridden. Still the dream of political engagement had taken hold.

NOTES

1) The concept of 'Shepherding' arose out of a concern for effective discipleship and put great emphasis on the need for submission to spiritual leaders. In an article of the history of the charismatic movement, pastor Gary E Gilley writes: "Shepherdship is an oppressive system in which a person who often perceives himself as an immature Christian submits himself to the leading of an 'elder'. The elders (shepherds) are appointed in much the same way as in other hierarchies, with one submitting to the next higher in a chain of

command. Total discipline is imposed on those who submit themselves to an elder. His leadership is total, even extending over the person's family life. Failure to obey the shepherd can lead to disapproval, verbal condemnation, and ultimately being put out of the fellowship. The most significant aspect of the unbiblical shepherding system is that one person submits his will completely to another individual, the shepherd or elder."

2) From Monday 28 January (1984-1986 journal).

3) Martin O'Brien, *Belfast Telegraph,* November 1981.

4) Further to Nigel's problematic encounter with the word 'Church' (see p58) it is interesting to note David Matthew's comment. "Church has been one of our differences. Des and his folk believe that the true church is essentially the Roman Church and that one day we will all have to join; he adds the rider that it will be so changed by then that we could readily come in. I believe that the Church is yet to be built on earth and that one day all labels, including Roman Catholic, will have to be dropped. Meanwhile, we get on with the pragmatics and leave some of the eschatology in God's hands." David Matthews, 'Sins of the Fathers', Belfast Christian Family, 1981.

5) David Matthews, 'Sins of the Fathers', Belfast Christian Family, 1981, Leaflet 8, p4.

6) Notebook 1981-82 (This is a slightly shortened version of the full text under an entry dated 13 April 1982).

CHAPTER SEVEN

HATCHED

FIFTEEN MONTHS LATER NIGEL penned a ten page paper entitled 'A Political Career'. It reads like a personal manifesto and would act as a strategic blueprint for many years to come.

"This note sets out some thoughts and aspirations which I have harboured for a long time about the possibility of pursuing a political career," his type-script begins. "The reason I have put pen to paper on this subject is:

a) to clarify in my own mind why I should wish to enter politics;

b) to attempt to plan how the objective of entering politics might be fulfilled (as it will clearly not come about by accident or mere good intentions), and how other priorities in particular family life and church involvement, can be maintained;

c) to give the opportunity for others, and particularly the elders of the community to consider my idea, and help me evaluate whether they bear the hallmark of God's speaking and are realistically achievable."

He goes on to explain why he feels drawn to politics and to detail how he might enter the political field, which party he might join, the steps he would take to safeguard his family life, and how he foresees his ongoing commitment to Belfast Christian Family.

"I face a number of difficulties in pursuing a political career," he writes. "The most immediate and major problem is that as a Civil Servant involved in an administrative and policy job, I have been debarred from any political involvement for the last seven years, and would have to resign before I could take any active role in politics. I consider it virtually impossible to resign immediately before an election campaign, stand for election and be successful. I therefore believe that I would need to find a stepping stone between leaving the Civil Service and commencing a political career. Ideally this stepping stone should provide additional experience which would aid my political aspirations. My first preference would be to start my own business…"

—∞—

Hold the notion of Nigel starting his own business. Imagine it simmering gently on the back burner of his mind as he arrives in London, the following January, as part of the Belfast Christian Family leadership team. The leaders are there to confer with the leadership of a London-based ecumenical community with a view to joining an international federation of ecumenical communities known as Sword of the Spirit.

At this conference Nigel meets Louis Alexander. Probably most of us, looking back, can list a number of key encounters – apparently random meetings with particular individuals who somehow influence the subsequent course of our lives. It has been said, "You are the same today as you will be in five years time, except for two things – the books you read and the people you meet."[1] That's the way it was with Nigel and Louis.

In a break between meetings they got talking, quickly discovering how much they had in common – not least an up-beat, creative approach to challenge and a passion to see God act. Though Louis was some years Nigel's senior, they had children the same age. As they got to know one another, the conversation turned to careers and Louis created the spark that would blaze through the next five years of Nigel's life.

"So how do you earn your living?"

"I'm a civil servant," Nigel replied. "And you?"

Confident, suave, astute, empathetic, the man on the other side of the coffee table could easily have been cast as a doctor, a lawyer or a bishop. "I run my own business."

"What sort of business?"

"It's called InfoSound. We teach people how to use microcomputers and produce training materials."

"Oh really. I don't think there's anyone doing that in Northern Ireland."

Pause for a sharp intake of breath as mental curtains sweep back: Nigel surveys a fertile computer world which has just brought forth the IBM-PC. He sees companies beginning to buy into the benefits of information technology – an administrative revolution in the making. And what is this centre stage? His excitement rises. No business offering computer training in Northern Ireland? Surely it must be a great, inviting gap in the market.

The more he talked to Louis, the more the idea of opening an InfoSound sister company in Northern Ireland took hold. True, his computer expertise was limited. But in some senses that made the prospect all the more attractive. Nigel was always up for a 'new world' challenge. The adventurer in him longed to mount the back of this mighty technological wave approaching the commercial shore. Where he did not have a capability, he had confidence that he could quickly acquire it – or, perhaps more importantly, that as a Coordinating Prime Mover, he could find other people who did.

Now he had found Louis – a man who could supply him with all the know-how to make this sister act happen. Over the next few months Nigel prayed about it. He talked to Heather about it. He talked to David Preston and other community members about it. He talked to his work colleagues about it. He fleshed the idea out into a convincing business plan and talked to the bank and to LEDU (the small business agency for Northern Ireland) about it. All along the way people gave him a green light.

It's interesting to note how the philosophers and moralists of the eighteenth century placed great value in caution. "If you wish to succeed in life, make perseverance your bosom friend, experience your wise counsellor, caution your elder brother, and hope your guardian genius," advised Joseph Addison. Then along came the nineteenth century romantics throwing caution to the winds. Somehow, along with prudence and reason, caution never made a convincing comeback. The best-known contemporary quotations all counsel the leap into the unknown. Of these my favourite comes from CS Lewis. "It may be hard for an egg to turn into a bird:" he wrote. "It would be a jolly sight harder for it to learn to fly while remaining an egg. We are like eggs at present. And you cannot go on indefinitely being just an ordinary, decent egg. We must be hatched or go bad."

For Nigel not starting his own business would have been the equivalent to that unformed bird remaining a yolk. Heather totally supported him in this way of viewing things. She knew he'd felt all along that his employment in the Civil Service was temporary; that this urge to move on had been stronger than ever since his sense of call to 'activate politically'.

"We have talked about this subject on a number of occasions, going right back to before we even got engaged," Nigel wrote. "Even at that juncture I thought it was important that Heather should know of my political aspirations, and my hope that I could somehow affect the Northern Ireland situation. Heather responded positively then, as she does now…" [2] Indeed when asked how she felt about her husband turning his back on the secure income on which she and the family relied materially, Heather observed simply, "I've never wanted to live life in a rut."

Six months after his first conversation with Louis, Nigel left the Industrial Development Board to become Managing Director of the Province's first Computer Learning Centre. He spent the next six months setting the whole thing up. During that time he bought premises (on a prime site in the commercial heart of the city), state of the art equipment (hardware, software) and office furnishings. He employed staff... designed a logo... ordered stationery... planned his marketing campaign. He thought big and aimed high, all the while displaying meticulous attention to detail. At every point he received support from Belfast Christian Family (which had now assumed a new name, Community of the King, reflecting its wider Sword of the Spirit links). Some members invested in the business; some agreed to act as directors; on the London side, Louis gave generous encouragement, supplying training materials and advice; and when it came to filling the key post of Training Manager, Nigel only had to walk a hundred yards from his front door, to the home of community members, Roy and Kate Humphries.

An Information Technology (IT) expert, Roy taught computer science in a Technical College at the time. He remembers Nigel dropping in one evening to talk to him about the Computer Learning Centre and ask him whether he would consider coming on board. "He left me to think it over and discuss it with Kate," Roy recalls. "But to tell you the truth neither of us found it hard to make up our minds. I suppose at one level we knew it was a risk... but Nigel inspired confidence." Roy handed in his notice and that June came to join his new boss in the push to get the business up and running for the New Year.

—∿—

The business launch was scheduled for the second week of January.

Anyone who has ever launched anything knows the stomach-churning 'first night' feeling such occasions evoke. Excitement… panic… a hundred last minute details to attend to. Above all, the sense that this project into which you have poured yourself, body and soul, will finally be exposed to public view.

Picture Nigel, scribbling in a notebook, seeking a solid emotional and spiritual perspective on proceedings. "I have been planning for the business launch for so long it seems hard to believe it is actually happening," he writes.[3] "I sense that it is really important to operate from God's peace, particularly in giving myself to visitors and being an attentive host. I don't want to be so laid down with either busyness or anxiety that I am unable to effectively welcome people."

Twenty-four hours later, against the grain of her modest nature, Heather allows herself to be driven to Bulloch House in a gleaming stretch limousine (hired for the occasion by one of their 'cluster' neighbours). Visitors, including Louis and his wife Victoria, come from near and far. Nigel's marketing brainchild, Hero the talking robot, declares the Centre open. There are speeches by a local dignitaries, a full page advertising feature in that night's *Belfast Telegraph* and, crowning Nigel's publicity drive, like the mother-of-the-bride's hat, an item about the Computer Learning Centre on the local TV news.

What visitors saw when they entered the building was a state of the art training centre complete with an elegant reception desk, a seminar room, an executive suite and a training area with a circular sweep of training booths. Sets of headphones hanging on pegs on the side of each booth gave rise to a few queries. "That's how the training is delivered," Nigel would explain. "Every trainee is given an InfoSound pack, containing an audio cassette and training disc to talk them through their chosen course. This means you can come in, slot the audio cassette into position, put on your headphones and work away at their own pace. If you have any problems, it's like being on an aeroplane." With a flourish, he would press a button on the side of the nearest booth, illuminating a red light. "As soon as Roy sees that he'll be straight over to help you out."

The whole concept was both innovative and flexible. It had also required a heavy financial investment. At that time an IBM-PC, with a monochrome screen, a 64 kilobyte memory, two floppy drives and no hard drive cost £2000, and Nigel had bought around a dozen of them. The wordprocessing software, Wordstar, cost £600 to buy. Depending on the course selected, the training packs cost up to £100 and could not be reused. Within a very few years machines would become much cheaper and more powerful. One thing which Nigel had not foreseen was the speed with which these developments would take place. His instinct had been to spare no expense in getting the best equipment and creating the right image – cutting edge, professional yet user-friendly.

'Learn Wordstar on a DEC Rainbow or IBM PC,' 'Learn Visicalc on an Apple IIe', take 'an introduction to Microcomputing on an Epson PX8 or IBM PC', his advertising literature urged. In the buzz of excitement surrounding the high profile launch, nobody was talking about risk. But it was real and Nigel was aware of it. "The Lord is my security in the Computer Learning Centre," he had noted the week before the launch. "I realise that we are well past the point of no return." Already he was conscious that advance bookings were somewhat thin on the ground. Still he had confidence that this fanfare of publicity and goodwill would speedily translate into a steady stream of clients coming through the darkened plate glass doors.

NOTES
1) Charlie 'Tremendous' Jones (see www.executivebooks.com)
2) From 'A Political Career?', 27 July 1983.
3) From Monday 14 January 1985 (1984-86 journal).

CHAPTER EIGHT

MONEY AND MIND MAPS

OUTSIDE THE SUN HAS pulled down its shutters for the day and twilight lurks around the city corners. Suit jacket off, tie loosened at the neck, Nigel sits at his desk in the Computer Learning Centre (CLC), studying a spread sheet (run off courtesy of the latest Lotus 1-2-3 software). An uncustomary frown casts a shadow on his features. He can hear white noise – the gentle buzz of fluorescent light mingled with the hum of the computers. It is quiet – too quiet. He has worked hard all day – made phone calls, set up appointments, written letters. Until now experience has taught him that this kind of effort quickly pays off. But the spread sheet in his hands runs counter to everything he has known.

That sense of bemusement continues as he runs his eye down the printed columns on the page. He cannot dispute the figures. What does not add up is their message – the stark fact that received income for January has been significantly lower than projected.

Early February brings the good news that the Belfast-based aerospace giant Shorts may send people for training on a regular basis. Still weeks go by and Nigel, Roy and Tracey, the receptionist, often have the whole place to themselves, rattling around like well-groomed peas in a glossy high-tech pod. "This past week has been a real battle," Nigel writes as the month wears to a close. "Business has been slow. I found myself more intent on surviving the week than actually making concrete progress. The business was beginning to become a burden to me…"[1]

By the end of March, with yet another missed target to record, Nigel makes a mental adjustment. He recognises that this business he has created still does not have a momentum of its own. Despite the huge amount of time and energy it took to get it off the ground, he will have to keep pushing. "I find myself… wishing it will all land on a plate," he notes wistfully.[2]

"Welcome to the real world", the less-than-sympathetic observer might say. And truly for Nigel, this is a whole new order of experience. Up until this point in his life everything he has planted has sprung up and flourished. Still it isn't fair to say that nothing has prepared him for set-backs. Over the years he has identified closely with other people in their problems. Often, despite his (and Heather's) best pastoral efforts, those problems have remained unresolved. He has shared burdens of frustration and failure – has encouraged others to not give up. And now he rises above his own discouragement. He reads the Old Testament Bible story of the Israelites conquering the Promised Land. "They still had to fight… That's what I need to hear… Mkting (sic) is not easy but we can succeed. Stick at it. Go for it." [3]

—⚊—

Cut to the Nevada Desert. Nigel and Louis are in a hired car marvelling at a spectacular lunar landscape bounded by the glorious pinks, rusts and greys of the distant mountains. They have motored from Las Vegas, home of the International Consumer Electronics Show. Here, too, they have seen marvels – microchips with five billion bits of information. As ever Nigel is fired by the possibilities… the implications.

"There are technological forces at work," Louis reflects. "Forces shaping the future, just as the forces of nature have shaped this dustbowl of a desert."

The sun burns low in the sky and they savour the sense of being on the creative cutting edge. There are fortunes to be made in the world of microcomputers – in developing, programming, in licensing, in retailing. This is, after all, the year when a young man the same age as Nigel will launch the first retail version of Microsoft Windows. But hitting the financial jackpot has never been Nigel's ambition. It strikes him that however his business develops, it isn't really about money any more than Las Vegas, for him and Louis, is about casinos. Money must never be his master. It's his servant. Money, as an end in itself, is meaningless. It must be kept in its proper place, viewed as a tool, not a goal.

—∿—

Another snapshot. Back in Belfast this time.

It's a typical Thursday and Nigel, en route to work, motors down the broad leafy University Road. He pulls in opposite the University. "OK Richard, see you later."

"Yeh, thanks." His passenger smiles a little distractedly and gets out.

Richard is a research student. He's found single life on a limited budget a struggle – but it has been a whole lot easier and happier since the Williams' took him in. He is very glad to be a temporary member (the first of many!) of this household and Nigel and Heather are glad of the opportunity to share their home.

—∿—

The threat of car bombs means no parking in the city centre. Nigel drives on towards town, then walks briskly from the car-park to the office. It's good to be out in the fresh morning air. Tonight is late opening in the CLC, so it's going to be a long day.

Things get off to productive start. With a cup of coffee at his desk, he reviews his priorities for the morning. He touches base with Roy... checks on bookings with Tracy and then moves into a telephone meeting with Louis in London. "There's no one like Louis," he would later record. "A jack in the box who keeps popping up again with some new idea… a tremendous encourager…"[4]

But by 3.00 pm everything has gone dead. Tracy tries to look busy. Nigel bites back frustration over a cancelled appointment. Roy is playing around on a computer.

"Hey, wait til you see *this*," he calls.

This is the IBM-PC storyboard programme which Roy has been using the afternoon lull to explore. Instantly Nigel is by his side, totally engaged with the discovery. If the acid test of a generous boss is whether you can say "Great, what a good idea" and really mean it, then it's a test Nigel passes with flying colours. "He always encouraged me to develop my skills," Roy recalls. "If things weren't busy in the Centre he was quite happy for me to play around with the computer programmes. He recognised the value of this."

At six o'clock there is a sudden burst of activity. No, not the elusive Shorts' trainees… or trainees from any other company for that matter. The visitors are the Williams family come to join Daddy for tea. Full of smiles, Kathryn and Simon, armed respectively with a book and a jigsaw, surge through the door. Two-year-old Linda follows with her doll, clutching Heather's skirt. The aroma of sausage stew fills the well-conditioned air. Nigel sees his pregnant wife, framed in the doorway, casserole in hand and his eyes light up with pleasure and pride. He might have the bank on his back and too few customers on the phone, but he has never been the sort of man to withdraw into his cave with a newspaper. Indeed, where some folk bring their work problems home with him, Nigel was always much more inclined, as this evening, to bring his family to work.

Amidst the wealth of human experience, one dominant strand remains grim and grey. Nigel's hard business slog continues with little to show for it except mounting debts. "I know I am in an impossible situation," he notes in June. "My back is against the wall. The world believes that what I want to do is out of the question. The banks are sceptical…" He goes on to express his faith that God will help him win through, concluding. "I'm concentrating on 'selling skills' but I believe God will help me with the bigger picture as well."[5]

This is something he really needs to hold onto as September gets under way. Initially things go reasonably well with a few thousand pounds worth of business in the first couple of weeks. The problem is the target for September is twice as high as August's and instead of the prayed-for increase there's a slump – a slump so marked that coming into the last week of the month Nigel isn't even sure if he will have a business in a few days time.

"Friday was <u>awful</u>," he records. "Appointments that were leading nowhere; cancelled appointments and so on." [6]

His next comment points up the faith that helped him bear the pressure. "Praise God for a busy weekend," he notes. "Late night stint on *Hap'nings*, Pastoral day, 2 meetings Sunday kept my mind off the problems. Indeed by Sunday night I really felt quite peaceful and joyous that the Lord new (sic) the way forward although I couldn't anticipate what was going to happen. I even felt like somehow the battle was won and decided not to adopt emergency fasting measures."

On Monday morning, still cloaked in an inexplicable sense of peace, Nigel steps into his office. Before he even has time to turn on the computer, the phone rings. A booking! He sets it down and almost immediately it rings again… and again… And so it goes on. For the next seven hours, the business pours in – just the way he has always believed it could. "Monday was incredible," he writes afterwards. "We made our target. With bookings coming from surprising sources… Hyster, BOE, UTV… we needed every one of them, but what a joy to see victory. Des and Les could hardly believe it. "How did you do it?" was their question. "Well, I know the Lord did it."

—⁄⁄⁄⁄—

If real life followed the patterns of fiction, this ought to have been a turning-point in Nigel's business fortunes. It doesn't and this wasn't. At the end of November he had something to celebrate – the safe arrival of his baby daughter Elizabeth, but it was a terrible month financially. Heather has recollections of sitting upstairs nursing the baby while an emergency board meeting went on in the downstairs lounge amidst the cards and flowers. "The need for a large injection of equity into the business at a time when we are fighting to get any customers at all produces plenty of scope for uncertainty, mental weakness and so on," Nigel wrote afterwards. "I have a whole range of initiatives planned for January requiring a lot of effort and I don't <u>want</u> to be double-thinking about the future of the business…"[7]

'Disappointment', 'frustration', 'losing my way' – these are the words which he uses to describe his feelings as 1985 draws to a close. These journal entries, however, are qualified by a series of mind maps. A mind map is defined as a diagram used to represent words, ideas, tasks or other items linked to, or arranged around a central key word or idea. "Today," says Roy, "mind maps are a key tool in modern management development training. Nigel was the first person I ever saw using them."

Nigel's mind maps reveal how he kept his negative work-related feelings in perspective. A mind map produced on 27 December shows the harassed Managing Director refusing to let the prospect of bankruptcy take the shine from his turkey dinner. Headed 'Priorities 1986 Non-business', it deliberately focuses on the big picture – Heather, the children, their wider family circle, the church community, his practical responsibilities, and political/ social concerns.

The diagram also demonstrates the fact that Nigel did not allow his business struggles to dull his social conscience. "Many of us… are small, disorganised and indifferent to any kind of evil that doesn't touch our lives directly," the psychologist Larry Crabb observes.[8] This could never be said of Nigel. Months previously he had noted that he and Heather were "very interested in CARE (Christian Action Research and Education) which is concerned with positive action in relation to social and moral issues."[9] In this particular mind map he prints the name 'CARE' in capital letters and sets it out on a branch of its own.

All too soon, though, the holiday season was over and it was time to address the mess. Nigel went back to work knowing that the physical building in which he and others had invested so much creative energy could easily become an empty shell… that the people he'd employed could become redundant… and that the responsibility was his.

As had happened so often before, his inner struggle brought him to David Preston's front door.

"Have you time for a chat?"

"Sure. Come in…"

"I'd rather go out." Somehow Nigel's questions seemed too weighty to be discussed in the familiar warmth of the Preston lounge. He needed somewhere different… somewhere less cosy…

So they walked into the dark chill of the January night.

It was a huge release for Nigel to pour out his feelings, to confess that he just couldn't rally the confused rabble of his thoughts into the orderly ranks of a positive plan anymore. The hardest thing was the sense that he had got something somewhere badly wrong – been misled by his own ambition, perhaps.

David listened. Then, matter-of-factly, he flagged up a wider dimension to the problem. "Many people believed with you, that God was calling you into the business world," he pointed out.

"If the business goes down," he added. "And you conclude that you heard wrong, a lot of other people did too."

In his view, however, the business was not so much a mistake as a battle-ground. "It could be there's a spiritual battle involved in winning through in the business. It's not just to do with your ability to bring in customers and make a go of it. Maybe you're up against something stronger... an enemy who does not want the Computer Learning Centre to succeed."

Obviously this is not the language of the board room. Company directors do not inform shareholders that poor returns are down to spiritual opposition. Many, though, may privately identify with the sense of being up against forces beyond human control. One thing is certain – David's unique blend of corporate solidarity and speculative metaphysics encouraged Nigel back into a position of faith.

What followed was a welcome but fragile season of profitability. Roy's skill with IBM's PC storyboard programme (a forerunner to Microsoft Powerpoint) developed into a commercial presentation service – whereby he and Nigel provided visual back-up (screened courtesy of an old-fashioned RGB projector) for conference speakers. They also discovered that companies often preferred to have training delivered on site. So they would pile fifteen machines into two estate cars and become a mobile computer suite. Overall the changes in work practice meant that the business could continue to operate out of much smaller offices and eventually the costly Linenhall Street premises was sold.

One way and another in the weeks immediately following his conversation with David, Nigel experienced an easing of financial pressure. Ultimate melt-down lay ahead but, in the medium term, prospects improved – an upturn reflected in the mind map which he sketched at the beginning of March. Whereas the December map looks like a diagram produced by someone determined to remind themselves that there are other things in life apart from work, the March sketch is much more integrated. One branch focuses on community relationships, a second is headed, 'consolidate business', a third, 'consolidate family life' and a fourth 'initiate politics'. Again attached to this branch is the significant little sub-heading 'CARE'.

NOTES

1) From Monday 25 February (1984-86 journal).

2) Ibid from entry dated Tuesday 26 March.

3) Ibid.

4) From 29 March (1989/90 journal).

5) From 10 June (1984-86 journal).

6) Ibid from 2 October 1985.

7) Ibid from 2 January 1986.

8) Larry Crabb, *Soul Talk: The Language God longs for Us to Speak,* Thomas Nelson, 2005, p56.

9) From Tuesday 5 February (1984-86 journal).

CHAPTER NINE

FOLLOWING THE STAR

REMEMBER THE LODE STAR? All through the ups and downs of Nigel's business venture, it has been there twinkling above his head. The dream of a seat in parliament. The call to 'activate politically.'

Now it guides him into a whole-hearted local involvement in the work of CARE. He starts speaking at meetings on their behalf, addressing social and ethical issues from a Christian standpoint. The star twinkles more brightly. He is appointed honorary national director for Northern Ireland. The star beams down with a reassuring glow.

Remember the Kallah players? (Answer – this was the drama group Nigel started up when he first returned to Northern Ireland and then let go.) Remember how he never wanted to keep doing something – even a good and successful thing – simply for the sake of it. "I don't want to get sucked into a self-perpetuating organisational mayhem,"[1] he once wrote. Any notion that he had hit a ceiling in terms of the strategic momentum of an activity quickly triggered an inner alarm bell.

Back in 1983 Nigel had mapped his career as follows: [2]
"Late 1984 / early 1985 - leave Civil Service for business career.
1985/86 - Develop business career, begin more open involvement in politics.
1987 - Stand for election, probably initially for a District Council.
1989/1990 - Possibly stand for election to Assembly (if there is one!) or to Westminster."

Now picture him waking up on New Year's Day 1987 – the year he had hoped to stand for election to a District Council. He is almost thirty-two years old. He has invested two and a half years in the Computer Learning Centre. He is playing a fruitful role in a whole range of arenas. But, rolling out of bed on the first day of a new year, with twelve strategic months ahead of him, all he hears is the disturbing jangle of that inner alarm. "You're in a cul de sac," it tells him. "You want to play the sort of political role that will make life better for the poor and socially disadvantaged. You want to shape policies relating to health, to education, to the arts and the environment. But here local politics are wedded to sectarianism. There is no place for you on the Northern Ireland political stage."

Then (metaphorically) he looks up. And yes, the star has definitely moved. It no longer twinkles above this strife-torn Province. It has shifted to the east.

"I start 1987 with one major issue on my mind," he wrote that morning, "the possibility of moving to London… There is virtually nothing in me that feels LONDON is the wrong thing for me at this time; indeed its almost as if I feel the decision has already been taken to go, and I want to get on with it… But there are certain things that will need to happen business-wise before we can move."(3)

Next morning this latter-day Dick Whittington talked things over with his wife. "Let's contemplate a second major change of direction in as many years – a change that will mean selling up, and saying goodbye to a special quality of life and relationship. We'll have to take our children out of good schools and a safe, supportive network of friendships and activities. It will mean building a whole new life in a big impersonal city." Those were the implications of what he said that day – implications to which flying saucepans or stony silence might seem a spouse's natural (and even justifiable) retort. Only one woman in a million, I suspect, would respond as trustfully as Heather did – listening, understanding, voicing her anxieties, but still, albeit reluctantly, open to the move.

"We reflected together (after some time of identifying Heather's concerns) on how the key issue is to follow God and how we have a secure life in him... and we have a solid family <u>core</u> which can be moved anywhere." Nigel was able to write.[4]

In part Heather's response was no doubt influenced by the emphasis the community placed on a wife's duty to submit to her husband – an emphasis balanced by their teaching on a husband's duty to show self-sacrificing love for his wife. But before feminist hackles rise, it needs to be said that Nigel would never have spiritually blackmailed Heather into doing something against her will. She shared his pioneering spirit – embracing challenge, accepting change.

A week later he approached David Preston and received a similarly positive response. "David was happy with our proposed move to London, and not too disbelieving that it might be this summer...," he records.[5] In terms of what he would do in London, Nigel envisaged working with Louis (they were already directors in each other's companies) while continuing to oversee the Computer Learning Centre which would employ a new managing director. In principal, both Louis and the other directors were agreeable to the scheme. But it all depended on both businesses – InfoSound and CLC – being secure enough to sustain the development. And this was problematic. On the one hand InfoSound had hit a rocky patch financially while in terms of premises and staff the Computer Learning Centre was in a state of transition. Nigel needed a buyer for the Linenhall Street building and some time in the next six months Roy Humphries and his wife would be moving to Malawi.

—⚬—

Nigel did not believe in destiny. He did believe in divine guidance. His God addressed people directly and revealed his will to them collectively and as individuals. The 'how to' of guidance was a favourite topic for Bible study groups. If asked, he would have gone along with the standard response that God guided his people primarily through the Bible, through strong impressions received in personal prayer, through wise advice from fellow believers, and through circumstances. Symbolic pictures, dreams and visions, messages in tongues and/or words of knowledge could be part and parcel of the process and, in exceptional cases, God might even guide through an audible voice or angelic intervention. Most importantly, though, Nigel held that any personal conviction about a course of action needed to be in line with general biblical principles, should be tested and approved by the wider body of Christ and would often receive circumstantial confirmation.

Therefore he welcomed the fact that before the move could go ahead certain factors beyond his control had to fall into place. As he saw it, this gave scope for divine endorsement. The London plan couldn't get off the blocks until he sold Bulloch House. When, twenty-four hours after his conversation with David Preston, a buyer turned up, Nigel heard the crack of a heavenly starter pistol.

Over the next few weeks the full extent of everything else that needed to happen became clear: the Computer Learning Centre required £100,000 worth of new business by mid-March, with £200,000 worth of capital being raised for InfoSound by the end of June. Nigel responded to the challenge with a joyful rush of confidence.

"This is really asking God for a very big catch but I have faith He can do that. No doubt about it." he wrote.[6] Past experience had taught him that orders could suddenly flood in. So he had every expectation that this would happen by the 17 March deadline. A slow week at the beginning of the month did nothing to dent this inner conviction. A second slow week was more testing. Still he did not lose heart.

Knowing this makes the non-event recorded in his diary entry for 18 March all the more poignant. "We didn't make the £100,000 yesterday," Nigel states baldly and then goes on to pick through the wreckage of his hopes.

"What am I thinking?

- Disappointed – this seemed a golden opportunity to move nearer to what I believed was God's plan – London, business, Louis and politics
- Not sure what the future holds. Need to reassess political and business objectives. Indeed, need to define these more carefully
- Niggle that one of the lessons I really need to learn is financial security and hard work and discipline in this area...

And yet, I have not given up on the dream..."

—⁓—

In some ways a non-happening – be it a non-healing, a non-pregnancy, a non-promotion, a non-romance – can be a particularly difficult blow. Those affected are generally expected to shake it off and carry on. Yet this is to gloss over the emotional trauma involved.

Nigel generally bounced back quickly from setbacks, but this one went deep. There was the loss of a clear plan; the loss of momentum; the loss of that exhilarating forward thrust in his spiritual life. It was as if a waveband had suddenly gone dead, forcing him to change frequency and tune into a message much less compatible with his natural inclinations – a message more about 'being' than 'doing', more about 'character' than 'action'. Now the words coming through in his Bible reading and prayer times, in his small group meetings and worship, were words like 'obedience', 'steadfastness' and 'financial discipline.'

It is hard to be obedient, steadfast and disciplined in the 'low' times of disappointment. During the remainder of the spring and on into the summer Nigel struggled with a loss of motivation, noting on one occasion that he "would be in grave danger of mentally toying with ditching lots of things at the moment – what folly."[7]

Still he persevered – with home improvements, with initiating new business, with supporting friends, with running a marathon, organising a conference and speaking at meetings for CARE. One thing he never appeared to do is doubt that there was a sovereign hand on his life. Instead he wrestled, rationalised, refocussed, confronted his perceived personal shortcomings. It all took effort and, from time to time – in the context of prayer and worship – he found, almost to his surprise, that he was wiping away tears.

That autumn the CARE organisation lost a key member of staff. "Mr Raymond Johnston, the director of CARE (formerly the National Festival of Light) died after a short illness on October 17," *The Times* obituary column recorded. "As director, he gave intellectual and political weight to a movement that had quiet but considerable influence... Much of his time was spent in research, writing, briefing and coordination of campaigns..."

Of course only those who had known and worked with the man could really perceive the organisational and personal crater he had left behind. Their grief would be ongoing... there was nothing to be done about that... but the immediate pressing problem was to find someone to step into Raymond's shoes.

Rene and Idwal's wedding day, 28 March 1951.

Nigel, not yet a year old, with his sister Sheila.

Susan has joined the family.

P2 at Limavady Primary School. Nigel is third from the left in the 2nd row from the back.

Setting the long jump record at Portadown College.

1st XV rugby team. Jacky Mulligan is on the left of the picture and Nigel far right of back row.

Part of the record Nigel kept of the trip to India.

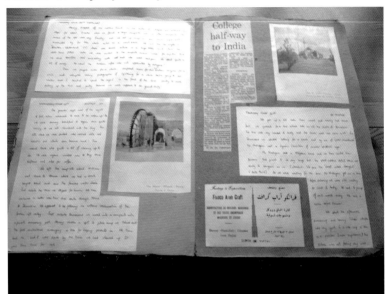

Student days 1973 (Nigel far left).

Downing College Cambridge.

Nigel (centre) enjoying a row on the River Cam.

Engaged May 1978.

The Williams' family at Nigel and Heather's wedding, 21 December 1978.

Nigel and Roy Humphries (left) with the head of IDB at the opening of The Computer Learning Centre.

Nigel and Heather with their children (from left) Kathryn, Elizabeth, Simon and Lynda on the eve of their move to London in May 1988.

A visit from friend and mentor David Preston, July 1989

Nigel with Lyndon Bowring, Lord Braine and Ann Winterton MP, 1989/90.

Family support for campaigning. Peckham, Spring 1994.

Winners of the 1st Childnet/Cable and Wireless Awards. London, January 1997.

1st Childnet Board Meeting in the new offices (from left) Tom Bick, Mike Hastings, Mike Conway and Mike Sheridan.

Larry Magid with Nigel 1997.

1st INHOPE meeting Amsterdam 1998

Prize winners in Paris 2002.

The year of the garden.

Lynda's wedding, July 2004.

NICCY offices in Belfast.

With Steve Carrick-Davis (right) and Will Gardner at the Namur Awards, January 2006.

Receiving the Namur Award from Penny Daqueonoy, January 2006.

A fun picture of Nigel with children at Foyleview School Derry, November 2005.

Back in Roe Valley Country Park for his 50th birthday with good friends Louis and Victoria Alexander and John and Helen (not in picture) Kyle, January 2005.

Enjoying a walk on Sallagh Braes with all the family, September 2005.

One October afternoon, seated at his desk in a windowless basement office, Lyndon Bowring, CARE's executive director, struggled to set their loss in the context of God's faithfulness. He reflected on the past. Over the fourteen years of its existence CARE had gone from strength to strength, declaring Christian truth in the public arena and practically demonstrating Christ's love. And in the present they had been blessed with wise trustees, gifted, committed staff and three superb honorary directors of the national movements – George Russell in Scotland, Rob Parsons in Wales and most recently Nigel Williams in Northern Ireland.

At the thought of Nigel – this clear-cut young evangelical so willing to work with all faiths and none – Lyndon brightens. Somewhere in the mound of paperwork on the desk he has a paper from his new Northern Ireland director – proposals for a CARE trust initiative on building up family life. He recalls that the carefully argued document had arrived on his desk at the end of January, not because Nigel had been asked to write it but simply because even in the midst of all his other administrative and organisational tasks, he had felt so deeply concerned about the issues he just had to sit down and unpack them.

Nigel, Lyndon reflects, would be the just the sort of person who might grow into Patrick's role. He smiles wryly… of course the notion is crazy. How could anyone expect a man, with a wife and four young children, to up-sticks and come and work for a lower salary in high cost London?

Still it was one of those crazy notions that somehow refused to go away…

––⁓––

Nigel's diary 28 October 1987

"The major development of yesterday was Lyndon approaching

me and saying had I thought of coming to work for CARE on the political side helping to put submissions to government, building up support within the political parties, researching and so on.

I was taken aback...

My reactions are – Lord – is this what you mean by activate politically?...

Three issues:

- Finance – I could not live and provide for my family on salary offered.
- Business – while the business is in a much better place it is still in a transitional phase – I have commitments to staff etc and Louis. How can I withdraw?
- Family/timing. I don't see how I can move before next summer...

Lord, these are big questions – I decided earlier in the year not to try and create the situation about London again but to respond to God's creating it for me. Is this it??"

—⁓—

The following Monday Nigel borrows a house. It belongs to fellow community members John and Averil Porteous – and they willing lend it to him for eight hours so he can have a quiet place to pray without interruption. Nigel has done something similar on a number of occasions throughout the year. Sometimes he's spent a day alone. Sometimes he's joined with one or two other men from his sharing group. The prayer days have been home-based, forest park-based and even car-based... but the aim is always the same – to dialogue with God and discern his will.

Nigel has rarely felt more in need of discernment than he does that cold November day. Should he or should he not accept the job with CARE? All morning he struggles; prays; leafs through Bible passages; flicks through a Christian magazine; prays again.

"I was tortured by doubts," he later recalled. "About housing. About how Heather would cope. About whether I could do the job. Or was I running away from business problems?"

And then, in the late afternoon, something changes. It is like emerging from a dark forest into a spacious, sunlit field. He hears an inner voice.

"Nigel what is the simplest question you need to ask?"

In this warm safe space, he can afford an unhurried reply – so he thinks for a while before answering, "the simplest question is – should I go?"

"Look at the story of Moses," comes the instruction.

Nigel opens his Bible. He is awed, expectant. And yes – there it is – a phrase from Exodus 3:10 leaping off the page at him. The simplest possible answer to his simplest question. 'So now **GO**.'

"Look at the story of Abraham."

He turns to Genesis 12:1 – and there it is again. '**GO** to the land I will show you.'

"And now look at Noah."

Genesis 7:1. For the third time in as many minutes the Spirit seems to highlight written words and make them into a personal instruction… '**GO** into the ark, you and your whole family.'

Just for good measure Nigel lifts the magazine he's been reading and his eye falls on the final sentence of an article by the charismatic Bible teacher, John Wimber.

"I'm scared half to death but I'll **go** with you Lord. I'll risk everything to **go** with you."

Whatever you make of this internal dialogue, one thing is undeniable. It was because he truly believed that he had heard God speak, that Nigel acted as he did.

On other occasions he would face decisions with a sense of the "gift of freedom God has given us," which he defines as "freedom to choose within the <u>liberating</u> constraint of God's challenge and values and plans for us"[8] – ie there could be more than one way to reach the destination and believers have a choice of route.

"God gave me a picture of the kind of order he doesn't want," he wrote.

"A prison – clinical, regimented order achieved by strict adherence to rules and regulations. He is more interested in exuberant order of a well-trained sports team, which has a plan to win the game but will set that aside if they see an opportunity to obtain the goal more quickly. The best disciplined teams can easily take advantage of these kind of openings."

In this instance, however, he maintained to the end of his life that he received a crystal clear instruction which called for a response of unquestioning obedience. "I had a very very powerful sense that I should go and that the means would follow," he told me.

So he stepped out in faith. With Heather's support, he accepted the post of Head of Care Campaigns – publicly burning his bridges. And this time the circumstantial confirmation *did* follow. A London businessman, Reiner Tholke, sympathetic to the work of CARE, had just sold his business. On hearing of the Williams' decision, he offered to help finance their relocation costs, making up the £85,000 difference between the price they could expect to get for Ladas Drive and the cost of an equivalent London home.

"Feel really privileged. I am walking on Holy ground!!" Nigel comments. "I need to let this sink in and understand what God is saying."[9]

Such understanding is hard to express. Undoubtedly there was a qualitative aspect to it – a growth in hope and faith. "The point I latched on to was not knowing why certain things had happened, finding God's ways hard to understand at times and yet trusting

God through it all much more for the future," he wrote that autumn.[10] But there was also a lesson about guidance – a lesson which Nigel continued to apply throughout his life in those times when he really needed to come to a decision and the way ahead was far from clear.

"You've got to go and talk to God," he would say. "But most of all you've got to listen and the most important thing you've got to do is work out the question you're asking."

NOTES
1) From Monday 6 April (1987 journal).
2) From 'A Political Career', 27 July 1983.
3) From 1 January (1987 journal).
4) Ibid from 2 January.
5) Ibid from Thursday 8 January.
6) Ibid from Wednesday 11 February.
7) Ibid from Tuesday 18 August.
8) From 8 May (2002 diary).
9) From Friday 27 November (1987 journal).
10) Ibid 2 October.

CHAPTER TEN

BEING A WATCHMAN

Nigel's Diary 26 May 1988

"LONDON! WE'RE HERE TWO weeks and I've been at CARE for a week. I'm feeling immensely challenged, provoked and keen to do the job to the best of my ability."

This is the opening entry in a diary that begins midway through the year and marks the start of a whole new chapter in Nigel's life. Then, as now, CARE was a mainstream Christian charity with thousands of supporters. Then, as now, it aimed to bring Christian insight and experience to matters of public policy and to take practical caring initiatives. Today the CARE offices occupy several floors of a high terrace building in the heart of Westminster. Back then Nigel initially commuted from the new family home in pleasant leafy West London to the basement of a vicarage in Mayfair. Victorian sewers beneath the floor-boards may have lent a certain 'fruitiness' to the office atmosphere, but mentally Nigel found the environment totally refreshing – everything he had hoped and more.

As Head of CARE Campaigns, his new role involved lobbying politicians about changes in legislation and managing the Campaigns team. It provided him with a pass to the House of Commons. It gave him access to politicians. It saw him scrutinising debates that had taken place on the green benches of the Commons and the red benches of the Lords. All in all it felt good – good in terms of what he hoped to achieve with CARE and good in terms of his ultimate goal of becoming an MP.

"The Houses of Parliament have an interesting impact on

visitors," he would say in a letter to CARE supporters. "Many are overawed by the sense of history, the archaic procedures and the technical language. Much of my work involves frequent visits to the House and meetings with MPs and Peers. I have discovered that Parliament is little different from any other human institution – a school governing body, a local council – and that the business of the House is remarkably open to influence if you know how to approach it. I do not think there is any magical secret to this. It is simply a case of learning the procedures and taking the opportunities..."

Reflecting on that learning curve, some five months into the job, Nigel sketched one of his characteristic mind maps. He entitled it 'being a watchman'. As a CARE staff member, his job was to watch over the government's legislative programme and critique its implications from a biblical standpoint. The idea was essentially positive. He aimed to support policies based on values that would promote a stable society with a respect for human life and oppose those that wouldn't. A major challenge lay in the fact that the work had to be done at one remove, through the good offices of sympathetic peers and MPs.

That autumn, under the direction of his boss, Charlie Colchester, and in the light of the parliamentary business set out in the Queen's speech, Nigel and his team laid their plans. A range of issues called for attention – issues which they also wished to resource groups of ordinary folk in every constituency to address at local level. In each of these areas CARE had an agenda which aimed to support the integrity of the family, the centrality of marriage and the sanctity of human life from conception. The issues included abortion, Sunday trading, embryo experimentation, education and pornography.

Meanwhile, back in the family home in affluent Boston Manor,

Heather was settling in. Each morning she heaved a sigh of relief as Kathryn, Simon and Lynda headed out to school without complaint. All along the children had viewed the move as a great adventure and now they seemed to be taking the transition in their stride. They shrugged off the inevitable 'funny accent' remarks. They brought friends home for tea. Without a paid employment role or a school routine to step into, their mother found the change harder. One thing that really helped, though, was the warm welcome they'd received in their new church fellowship.

The Williams had linked up with the West London Antioch Community [1], a sister fellowship to Belfast's Community of the King. Familiar faces included the Kyle clan, who had moved from Belfast to London some years previously. And then, of course, there were Louis and Victoria Alexander and their four girls. Despite the fact that they lived on the other side of London, the families had regular contact. Heather knew she had a great deal to be thankful for. Still, she had her low moments… especially at the thought of what life would be like when Elizabeth started school. What would she do then, she wondered? How would she spend her time? The very last thing she wanted was to sit about in a comfortable house in a nice area, twiddling her thumbs.

From October 1988 to April 1989 there is a gap in Nigel's diary. "The lack of written notes does not indicate a lack of prayer or study in the last six months," he helpfully notes. At work it had been "an important learning period, realising the honeymoon is over and beginning to build relationships."[2]

Some positive campaigning outcomes had included 400 copies of an Action Pack to combat pornography being sold to churches and local CARE Core Groups, and more than fifty MPs and Peers attending an anti-pornography seminar organised by the Campaigns team. Thanks to the seminar a number of MPs expressed an interest in working with CARE to tackle the problem of pornography generally and specifically change the law.[3] For Nigel, the honeymoon had ended in the sense that he now realised what a slow process this could be. It was like chipping away at the bottom of a cliff that would only come down when a majority of MPs present in the House for any vote were sufficiently convinced to accept the proposal. And equally he had to keep alert to the sound of chipping at the base of cliffs CARE wanted to keep intact – the statutes outlawing euthanasia for example. 'Being a watchman', in short, meant constant focused activity – often with few short-term rewards – chipping away and shoring up.

Another hard reality which surfaced during this post-honeymoon period was an inner tension between Nigel's lobbying on moral issues and his social/economic concerns. The CARE organisation as a whole, maintained a balance between practical caring and moral campaigning – but Nigel's job meant he had to focus on the latter. How, then, could he avoid a blinkered occupation of the moral high ground? He cared deeply about the biblical principles that underpinned the campaigns agenda. He also cared unconditionally about people and their human problems.

As he shaped up to campaign on a range of moral issues, Nigel acknowledged his deep human sympathies. "It's important not to delineate too narrowly certain issues as THE issues on God's heart," he notes. He senses that a simple life-style is somehow key to meshing his concerns – a simple life-style together with a will to help. He and Heather share a deep desire to reach out to 'have nots' in society. "We will not be rich (in terms of possessions) but the Lord will meet our needs and enable us to serve the poor. The issue of single parents doesn't go away from my mind." [4]

With anyone else that sort of a comment could end up permanently filed away in a 'Good Intentions' folder. With Nigel it sends out a signal – watch this space.

NOTES

1) The Antioch Community is an ecumenical, charismatic fellowship which began in the early 1980s with the encouragement of the Catholic and Church of England dioceses in London. Members attend their own denominational churches on Sunday mornings and then meet together on Sunday afternoons and mid-week in small groups. Nigel and Heather remained fully involved in this group for almost thirteen years until responsibilities in his local Anglican church meant Nigel could no longer sustain this level of commitment.

2) From 3 April 1989 (May 1988-April 1989 journal).

3) The 1959 Obscene Publications Act had defined obscenity as "something likely to deprave or corrupt" – which made it so hard to prove a given publication was obscene as to practically rule out all likelihood of a successful prosecution.

4) From 3 April 1989 (May 1988-April 1989 journal).

CHAPTER ELEVEN

OVERCOMING THE EXPECTED

As a couple, the Williams had stepped out into 1990 with two main desires. First, to find "some new work of mercy... some means of loving others" for Heather to pioneer. Second, that Nigel should find greater scope for service in political life. Certainly he relished his employment as political lobbyist – the challenge to persuade, the opportunity to put words into honourable members' mouths. But how much better if he could stand up in the Commons and speak them for himself?

Many of the briefings he wrote at that time – drafts of which littered the floor of his Romney Street office – dealt with the 1990 Human Fertilisation and Embryology Bill then making its way through parliament. It had been designed to legislate for three main activities: fertility treatments involving the use of donated eggs, sperm or embryos created outside the body; the storage of eggs, sperm and embryos; and research on early human embryos. For CARE the Bill threw up a raft of 'family life' and 'sanctity of human life' related issues.

Work had its lighter moments – such as the occasion a supporter kept a long-suffering staff member on the phone for forty-five minutes stridently foretelling hail, rain and flood. "I believe there is someone in your office with earache," was her parting prophetic shot. Nevertheless it was exacting. By this stage the five person Campaigns Team (Nigel, Luke, Janice, Jane and Lesley) had really gelled together. Theirs was a comradeship forged at a recent Tory Party conference, in accommodation reminiscent of Fawlty Towers, miles from the conference centre and without a towel between them.

This intrepid group lobbied for experimentation on embryos to be prohibited, for birth certificates involving the donation of sperm or ova to include the words 'by donation', for children to have the right to discover the identity of their genetic parents and for an amendment bringing the time limit on abortions down from 28 to 24 weeks. To these ends they scrutinised, analysed, researched, communicated, briefed, publicised, drafted and redrafted amendments. They organised the launch of Care for Life in the Royal Albert Hall. In short they gave the campaign everything they'd got. They were, as Luke later put it, "firing on all cylinders with every member playing to their own strengths".

During the last week of March, just prior to the Human Fertilisation and Embryology Bill's second reading, Nigel left behind the minutiae of clauses and amendments to take a short break in Barton-on-sea. Remember that retreat to Barton-on-sea? This is the point where he strode along the beach, watching the gulls and recalling people, like Jackie Mulligan, who had encouraged him to ride high.

Later that same day Nigel took a second walk across the sand. Unbidden, a sentence sprang to mind. "Following God involves overcoming the expected in order to achieve the important." He thought of the things the world expected of a 'successful' man at his stage in life: wealth, status, pleasure, security, possessions, achievement. It struck him that decision-making could so easily be shaped by these expectations – expectations that must be overcome to achieve life's best. And as he walked the words of a prayer welled up from deep within his being: "Lord, help me to not just talk about longings and never get there. Talk about poverty but never be poor. Talk about politics but never be a politician. Lord fulfil your word – and may I know it's been fulfilled."[1]

―᚜―

The diary note Nigel wrote that first day detailed his heart's desires. The following day brought a visionary thrust towards achieving them. On the afternoon of 30 March he became engrossed in the biblical account of King David. Sixteen chapters into the story came God's message to the King about his desire to build a Temple. 'God says don't you think about building a house for me,' (v5) Nigel read. 'The Lord declares to you that the Lord himself will build a house for you' (v2). 'I will raise up your offspring to succeed you' (v12).

Suddenly he could read no further. The sentences enthralled him.

"I know that "house" means lineage," he comments in his dairy, "but it also has the connotation of building."[2]

House... offspring... opportunity... future...

Minutes passed. Minutes pregnant with excitement. Ideas and associations coalesced and a whole new picture filled his mind. In the foreground was the memory of a conversation he had with one of the Antioch leaders the previous Sunday. Iain had referred to a spiritual leading which had prompted some of the younger members to consider buying property in the inner city area of Peckham. Now this almost casual reference came back to him in glorious technicolour. It was illuminated by Heather's desire for a new area of service and by their mutual commitment to a radical life. It involved a house – a house in Peckham. "God wants to provide a house that will be a base (perhaps... for Heather to exercise her haven ministry.)" In the middle distance Nigel saw his family as part of an Antioch cluster relocating to this needy part of London. And he saw Simon, Kathryn, Lynda and Elizabeth – his lineage house – happy and safe. Peckham might not be the sort of area where most people would choose to buy property. But Nigel believed God was promising to protect and watch over his children "even if the circumstances are not good."

Nine months later seven-year-old Lynda skips over to her school-teacher, her small face flushed with excitement. "My mummy and daddy have bought a new house. It's in…um…" with a smile of triumph she pulls out the word, "Peckham. We'll be moving there very soon. And me and Elizabeth and Kathryn and Simon, we'll be going to new schools. And Daddy says Simon can get a dog…"

"That's enough, dear," the teacher interrupts. "You shouldn't go making up stories."

But of course the story wasn't made up. The nine months since Nigel's retreat to Barton had been marked by a series of highs and lows. One major low had arisen from the defeat of the Campaign Team's Embryo Bill battle on almost every front. Experimentation on embryos got the go-ahead – with a minor gain in the form of an amendment stating that before fertility treatment was provided, a child's need for a father should be taken into account. The upper time limit on abortions had been lowered from 28 weeks to 24. But the team's relief turned to dismay with the dawning realisation that that the net effect of a further series of technical amendments had made it legal, in certain circumstances, for abortions to be carried out right up until a baby was full term.

At one level Nigel had still been numb with disappointment on the bright June evening when he and Heather had got together with a few others to pray about the Peckham vision. Emotionally it would have been so easy to let it go – easy, that is, until the whole tone of the gathering unexpectedly altered. The sceptic would probably call it mass hysteria – except the half a dozen folk involved could hardly be counted a mass. As they saw it, the Holy Spirit stepped in.

"I got stuck in my armchair with my hands raised rigidly unable to move them," Nigel records. At the same time Heather heard the Lord say, "Don't put your hand to the plough and then look back." In the weeks that followed three other families committed themselves to the same furrow.

"And so gradually we edged towards moving (to Peckham). At times filled with doubt but knowing we should press on. We became regular visitors to the area looking at houses and schools... In December we looked at a particular house directly opposite the (Pelican) estate. We began to make enquiries about selling our own home. Then in mid-January everything started to happen. In the space of two weeks we had our offer accepted on the house we had visited; we sold our own house; and Kathryn was offered a secondary place in our first choice school. We were amazed at God's hand in it all and the speed of the action. It was obvious we should move sooner than we planned, at Easter 1991 rather than the summer."[3]

—∾∾—

On 31 March, almost one year exactly after Nigel's retreat in Barton, the Williams took possession of 14 Talfourd Road. To the watching world April Fools Day might have seemed a very fitting date for their first full day in their new home. Indeed the fact that Lynda's news had sounded so unlikely to her former school teacher indicated the extent to which the first part of Nigel's Barton beach prayer about 'overcoming the expected' had been fulfilled. No-one expected a nice, middle-class family to relocate too run-down Peckham. But if Nigel and Heather were fools in any sense, it was in the biblical sense of being 'fools for Christ's sake.'[4] And they hadn't operated alone. John and Jenny Campbell and their children, Peter and Jessica Greedy and Mike and Jane Hastings had bought property close by. A team of nineteen Antioch members rolled up their sleeves to help the family shift their worldly goods. Typically Nigel lists each name, commenting, "We made it (with a lot of help from our friends)".

"Since arriving here both Heather and I have felt 'at home'", he goes on. "The house is bigger and lighter than I remember it… The garden has a lot of character and the children really like it. Our room is especially big and will be a good study area."[5]

Little did he realise how vital it would prove to have that extra bedroom space – not to mention a very large attic – in their newly acquired Victorian terrace home. At this point, after so much upheaval, he is content for once simply to draw breath and go with the flow.

"The question is why are we here?" his diary entry concludes.

All he knows so far is that he and Heather and the other families have come to Peckham "to construct a haven in our home, to create community…" He's aware that these are big generalisations. But that's enough for now. It's like opening one of Lynda's activity books and finding pages and pages of outline figures, waiting to be coloured in.

NOTES
1) From 29 March (1989/90 journal).
2) Ibid.
3) From an entry entitled 'The Pelican Project' (Dec 90–April 91 journal).
4) 1 Corinthians 4:10.
5) From 1 April (Dec 90–April 91 journal).

CHAPTER TWELVE

MAELSTROM OF ACTIVITY

READING THROUGH THE DIARIES Nigel kept in his Peckham years one senses pressure. These are notebooks filled with hastily written observations, prayers, Bible verses, mind maps and 'to do' lists. "Home exhausted."

"Go… go… go…"

"Frantic at work"

"Three solid days of madness."

"My in-tray has built up again – ugh!"

"So another impossibly busy week – O just to draw breath!"

And then, from amongst the foolscap pages, a loose sheet falls out. I pick up a brightly coloured childish drawing. A basket of gold-centred pansies – blue, tourquoise, magenta and black – a treasured gift to Daddy.

That glowing little memento holds me. "In many ways for the next 10-15 years the children are the priority," Nigel noted on his thirty-eighth birthday, twenty-two months after the move. "Seeing them established securely and hopefully in faith. I don't mean financially secure but emotionally secure…"[1]

There's poignancy in the realisation that when he articulated this desire for the next fifteen years, he actually did not have as long as that to live; there's awareness of the wider significance of his words – for children all over the globe would indeed be his priority. Then there is the happy recollection of conversations with Kathryn, Simon, Lynda and Elizabeth illustrating how, throughout the intensely busy season which followed, he fathered them consistently and creatively, leaving a host of treasured memories between the pages of their lives.

The junior Williams' Peckham years saw them play musical instruments, act in school plays, join uniformed organisations and youth groups, and get top grades in exams. Of the four, Lynda and Elizabeth rooted most deeply in the locality, but they all formed close friendships with other children both at school and in the Antioch community. Simon remembers father and son cycling trips and cricket matches in London; Kathryn remembers being taken to see *A Midsummer Night's Dream* in Regent Park, an outing complete with a picnic of raspberries and pork pie beforehand. Elizabeth has memories of a special train-trip to the seaside. Lynda vividly recalls an outing to the circus where, typically, Nigel had arranged for ring-side seats and ended up with a starring role in the clowns' knife-throwing act.

It's sobering to think that in Peckham the knives were truly threatening. The family had moved to an area where the housing developments of the sixties had produced a warren of low-rise council properties which, by the late eighties, had become notorious sink estates, characterised by burglaries and illegal drug dealing. Long before the tragic murder of ten year old Damilola Taylor hit the headlines, everyone knew the risk of violent crime. Even so, the Williams children felt safe and settled.

In October 1993 Nigel sent out a circular letter subtitled 'News from the Peckham Cluster of the Antioch Community' . In it he refers to the various ways which had opened up for the families who had moved the area to make a local contribution.

Heather has become active in a church-based initiative called PECAN (Peckam Evangelical Churches' Action Network), which aims to tackle unemployment within the sink estates. Jane Hastings has established a charity, Springboard, equipping volunteers to give one to one teaching to school children who cannot read or write.

Under the umbrella of their local Roman Catholic church, John and Jenny Campbell are involved in an outreach to the poor and needy, the Neo-Catechumenate Way.

As for Nigel himself, after seven years of slippage, his political ambitions are back on track. The most significant development since the move to Peckham has seen him joining the Liberal Democrats and being selected to stand for Southwark Council in May 1994. His earnest request for prayer "for endurance in all the work involved: preparing literature, delivering it, raising money and canvassing" masks a well spring of excitement.

—⚌—

"Vote Alden! Vote Bernadt!" In the run down to the District Elections, the sitting labour candidates for Lane Ward, Peckham, confidently expected to see off all contenders. Councillors Alden and Bernadt had every reason to believe their seats on Southwark Council were safe. Peckham had been a labour stronghold for decades. Four years previously they'd outpolled their nearest conservative rivals by almost a thousand votes. They could be forgiven for regarding their Lib Dem challengers rather as picnickers regard flies. "Sarah Harrison and – who? – Nigel Williams. Oh, you mean the bald Irish guy, with the moustache. New to the area, isn't he?"

It's easy to underestimate a newcomer – especially when you don't have first hand experience of aforesaid newcomer's coordinating ability and creative drive. By early May the Harrison/Williams team had delivered an amazing 20,000 leaflets. Almost every evening for four weeks Nigel (often accompanied by daughter Elizabeth) bounded up and down stairwells, stuffed leaflets under doors and, with his trademark twinkling gaze, tried desperately to engage folk in conversation. He even sailed through the Rye Lane shopping precinct, standing upright on the front seat of a space cruiser, head and shoulders poking through the sun roof. "Vote Liberal Democrat!" His voice crackled gallantly through a hand-held megaphone. Bemused shoppers halted, open-mouthed, in their tracks.

Why Liberal Democrat? This is not the shoppers' question – it's mine. The main clue, once again, is found in his 1983 strategic blueprint, which contains the following observation under the heading 'Which Party?'

"In years gone by there was a gallant group of members both in Stormont and Westminster, with the 'Independent' tag. Nowadays it is extremely difficult to get elected without some form of party political tie. If I were in Great Britain I might end up in the Liberal/ SDP fold or possibly on the left of the conservative fold."

He goes on to bemoan the sectarian nature of Party politics in Northern Ireland. With a certain youthful disdain, he considers his options as a choice between "risking standing as an independent" and "seeking to add backbone to the Alliance Party". He even toys with the idea of starting his own Family and Community Enterprise party.

The FACE party notion swiftly faded. Not so the party political leanings. Seven years later, on one of the many occasions when Nigel set out to fathom "the next steps... in political life," he would note "my conviction about going Liberal Democrat is increasing."[2] Still there continues to be a sense that his choice of party is as much a matter of political necessity as ideological conviction. Nigel felt called to be a politician first and a Liberal Democrat second.

Once he came into the fold, though, no party leader could have looked for a more committed local activist. Nigel, and his Lib Dem running-mate Sarah, entered the ring like the proverbial breath of fresh air. So what if the odds were stacked against them? "Our campaign was classic Liberal Democrat and classic Nigel,"

Sarah recalls. "It was about local action on local issues, helping people locally. It was also excellent, excellent fun." She remembers fundraising barbecues in the Williams' back garden, Nigel as 'quiz master supreme' on the top floor of the Old Nun's Head Pub on Nunshead Green.

"A good day's campaigning," Nigel notes at the end of his busiest ever May Day holiday. "Lord, will we win? A lot of people expect us to but can't be sure. It's going to be down to the wire…"[3]

That Thursday he discovered that his and Sarah's unique mix of energy, personality and clear policies (not to mention that space cruiser) had done the trick. "We had a 'humming' polling day," he notes. "Covered every polling station… wonderful reaction from people… somewhere along the line we had caught people's imagination…"[4] To their chagrin, the two labour counsellors didn't romp home after all. Instead they saw a small significant dot of yellow push its head up through the sea of red. Their safe labour seats were snatched from under them. Harrison and Williams topped the poll.

––⁓⁓⁓––

What the electorate did not know was that Nigel's successful public campaign had taken place against a backdrop of private tragedy. One black week in March had brought the shocking news of the death of Heather's older brother Ernie. Two days after the funeral, before Heather had even had time to unpack her clothes, let alone begin to come to terms with her loss, she received a second heart-breaking phonecall. The news this time was that her sister Angela had suffered a major heart attack and now lay comatose in hospital.

Days… weeks… months went by. Angela's condition remained unchanged. Nigel fought his election campaign and came out the other side. But for Heather there could be no such relief. Within a matter of days she had effectively lost a brother and an elder sister who, since the early death of their own mother, had been like a mother to her. It was one of those tragic situations which seem to drag on cruelly and senselessly with no hope of resolution.

What this meant was that when Nigel came in through his front door each evening, he had a choice. Either he could go through the motions of domesticity, while mentally remaining at his desk – or he could ask his wife "how was your day?" and really care about her response. The second option was not easy, as anyone with work preoccupations will understand. But Nigel chose it. When he walked through that door, he was truly there – there to draw Heather out, to listen when she wanted to talk, to give her space when she needed to withdraw. Perhaps most importantly he was there not to short-circuit her grief or to impose pat answers, but to share her emotional pain.

—m—

So we come to the autumn of 1994 – a time when Nigel has the equivalent of two full time jobs. In CARE, his day job, work is varied and demanding as ever. He has been appointed 'Head of Public Policy.' Over the past three years, amongst numerous other things, he has prepared a report for the Department of Home Affairs on computer pornography; helped pave the way for the granting of licences to specifically Christian radio stations; overseen the establishment of CARE's highly successful parliamentary intern programme; and helped ensure the retention of the Metropolitan Police's Obscene Publications Squad. He has also has written one book on pornography[5] and had another commissioned[6].

On Southwark Council – his evening job – there's an average of four committee meetings per week. On top of this he spends hours helping individuals sort out problems with bureaucracy. He works to resolve conflicts in the community. He has surgeries and meetings with local residents, makes phone-calls, attends civic events and ploughs through stacks of paperwork. Any sense of drudgery is outweighed by the sense of progress. With a huge inner-city regeneration programme in the offing, Nigel knows he is ideally placed to help bring about a sea-change in Peckham's five sink estates.

Then, just when it seems things can't possibly get any busier – they do. The decorations go up. The fairy lights are turned on. It's the week before Christmas – with letters to write, presents to buy, nativity plays to applaud.

"My life (or lives)", he comments accurately, if inelegantly, "is a maelstrom of activity." And in that maelstrom he fears he is losing his sense of strategic direction. He feels swept along by a multitude of demands.

"Lord harness the power to a constructive direction," he prays. "So that initiatives will be productive. Life is complicated but you are God. I desire to move with your Spirit and allow you, Oh Lord, to create from our lives the purposes that you wish to (fulfil). Father, I sense your timing… your hand…"[7]

Cut to a spacious, well appointed hotel bedroom overlooking the bright lights of Melbourne city. Nigel sits at a desk, writing feverishly. It's the dead of night. Still the air on the balcony outside is warm. He has left behind the January smog for the delights of an Australian summer. The first World Conference of Religious Leaders on Pornography will be held in Manila the following week. Nigel and his CARE colleague Claire Wilson-Thomas are booked in. To make the most of this trip to the Southern Hemisphere he has come a few days early and scheduled meetings with various groups in Melbourne and Sydney on CARE's behalf. Heather, meanwhile, is in Perth. While he confers, she is spending two weeks with Stewart, the brother she hasn't seen for over twenty years – something which, in the light of the tragic events of the previous year, will surely do them both good.

The streets outside are as quiet. The king-size bed in Nigel's room is luxuriously inviting – pillows plumped high, sheets turned back. Guests, all over this gracious hotel, are sleeping peacefully. Nigel sets down his pen and rubs his eyes. They are gritty with tiredness. He wants to close them but knows they won't stay shut. He has showered, spoken to Heather on the phone, made detailed notes of the day's meetings. There's not another thing that he can do until morning. Still he sees no point in lying down. It's less than a month since he prayed for constructive direction in the maelstrom of activity, and today he has been possessed by an idea. It is gripping him, wooing him, filling him with excitement. But before he dares to entertain it, he needs to be sure...

He picks up his pen again and flips open his diary.

"MELBOURNE – unreal existence in beautiful hotel," he writes. "Completely time zone zonked. Not sleeping. Beset by idea for International Institute for Content Standards on the Information Superhighway. Father, Lord, is this of you – or is it a <u>mad</u> dream?... Lord, sift me."[8]

Ten days later he's nursing a coffee in Bangkok's Don Meuang airport. He has caught up on his sleep but the 'mad' idea has not gone away. If anything, the reports and discussion in Manilla have strengthened his sense of call. The big question is when should he broach the subject with Heather. He glances at his watch. She'll be joining him any minute now for the journey home. He's bursting to tell her but the timing has to be right. There are other things they must talk about first. Perhaps fifteen or twenty minutes into the flight... when she's had a chance to relax...

Mentally he rehearses the conversation.

"How was the conference?" she will ask.

"*Very* interesting," he will reply with careful emphasis. "It really brought home to me the dangers of pornography on the Information Superhighway..."

This may produce a questioning look. He's pretty sure she'll know what the Information Superhighway is... but on the other hand, she may not...

"Remember... we've talked about it... it's a way for students to get information without entering a library... a global communication network through computers. It's big and getting bigger. People can send messages to each other... not just words... but photographs. It's a wonderful tool but there are dangers... especially for children And... well..." He knows that here he must try to sound measured... not let his voice squeak with excitement. "The thing is I think I'm meant to do something about it..."

"What sort of thing?" she will say. "You're already working on a book. Isn't that what your book with Claire is about?"

"Partly," he'll reply. "But I think I'm meant to do more than write a book."

"You mean a CARE campaign?"

"More than a campaign," he'll take her hand. This is the key moment. She's going to need reassurance. "I really believe I should leave CARE and work at this full-time... raise funds... start a charity... I've been praying and praying and the idea just seems to get stronger all the time... So what do you think?" At this point Nigel ditches the inner dialogue. He hasn't a clue how his wife will respond. More importantly he has spotted a familiar figure pushing her baggage-laden trolley through the crowd.

"Heather!" He races forward, arms outstretched.

And now they are seated side by side in the plane. The conversation is taking place – though not as rehearsed. The mad idea just comes tumbling out of him: this amazing communication system, the fact that no-one is looking out for the interests of children, his sense of call to do something about it...

So what *does* she think?

He squeezes her arm and Heather meets his eyes. She sees them sparkling with that familiar mix of excitement and drive. She trusts his judgement. She really wants to share his enthusiasm. Still her stomach churns.

"Nigel," she says bluntly. "Will it mean moving house?"

And this time, to her great relief, the answer is "no".

NOTES

1) From 21 January (1993 journal).

2) From Tuesday 30 April (Dec 1990–April 1991 journal).

3) From Monday 2 May (1994 diary).

4) From Thursday 5 May (1994 diary).

5) Nigel Williams, *False Images – Telling the Truth about Pornography*, Kingsway, 1991.

6) Claire Wilson-Thomas and Nigel Williams, *Laid Bare: Path Through the Pornography Maze*, Hodder and Stoughton Religious, 1996.

7) From Sunday 18 December (1994 diary).

8) From Friday 13 January (1995 diary).

CHAPTER THIRTEEN

GOING GLOBAL

THE PLANE LANDS. It's back to earth with a jolt – back to jet lag, back to the disturbing news that Simon has been attacked in the street (thankfully losing nothing more than his wallet) back to playing 'catch up' at the office. As ever, CARE's Public Policy Department is all go. At one level it is business as usual; at another, the idea of doing something about children and the Information Superhighway continues to dominate Nigel's thoughts.

One Monday, at the beginning of February, he fleshes the concept out – the silver lining to the cloud of a viral infection. He might have a small bonfire smouldering at the back of his throat which turns into a blazing inferno when he swallows, but that doesn't stop him typing. He sits down at the computer and the first draft of his Internet paper flows up onto the screen.

"Imagine if paedophiles could take pictures of child abuse in SE Asia and transmit it (sic) to accomplices in Britain minutes later with little chance of detection," a later version of the document reads. "Suppose children could see the most horrific pornography in their bedrooms without their parents knowing. *This is not imagination – it is already happening...* Known as *'the Internet'* this worldwide communications system has very little regulation..."[1]

A pause is called for here – just to acknowledge, once again, Nigel's foresight. Indeed if you were looking for one phrase to sum him up, I would offer the words, 'he got there first'. In 1995 most people had little inkling of the communication revolution that lay ahead, never mind any thought of its implications for children.

Nigel got there first. He proposed to establish what he then referred to as an 'international research centre' to protect children's interests as the new technology developed. It was also clear to him from the outset that there could be no effective monitoring and policing of a global medium without international cooperation – so the 'international' dimension was central to what he had in mind. But he wanted to do more than simply protect children from harm. He saw the body developing practical uses of the Internet to empower children and show them the benefits of worldwide communication. Making the Internet "a great and a safe place for children" was the catch-phrase he later used to sum up these twin thrusts.

The document ends with a price-tag – a budget of £500,000 per annum. "The immediate challenge," its author concludes, would be "to raise £150,000 pump priming assistance to draw in support from the computer industry and Government."

Let's step back again in time for a moment. Shortly after the Williams' move to London in 1988, Nigel's first business venture, the Computer Learning Centre, hit the rocks. As a director he had watched it founder. He saw the employment crisis it created in the life of the friend who had taken over as managing director. He had been left with debts and worse – a sense of responsibility for other people's debts. Some friends in the then Belfast Christian Family had borrowed significant amounts of money to put into CLC – and lost it all when the company went bust. "I never heard anyone regret doing it," the chairman of the CLC board would say. "It was just a part of being family – supporting and caring for each other." Still the whole episode had left Nigel with the bitter taste of a failure he found hard to accept and even harder to understand.

Journal entries from that period give some insight into his

thinking. "Success is not promised in the Scripture," he notes. "Perhaps Paul's statement is the critical one, 'I have learnt to be content in all circumstances'... to seek to answer questions, to journey with the right attitude is sometimes more important than arriving..."[2]

It is telling, in the light of this struggle, that Nigel is prepared to repeat the risks of the past. He knows now that a strong sense of call is no guarantee of success; that no matter how hard, how prayerfully, how creatively you work, you can be left with a sense of missing the mark. He has faced hard business realities and knows, in a way those in more sheltered occupations can only imagine, the sheer challenge of holding to principles of truth and integrity in the cut-throat world of 'the Apprentice'. Undeterred, early summer 1995 sees him sitting with a group of men in the front room of his home, ready once again, to step out as a social entrepreneur.

The men are the prospective trustees of the embryo 'international research centre', now named Childnet International. Ten years previously Nigel had sat with a similar group making plans for the CLC. Once again these are all folk who understand 'the song of faith' that drives him – men drawn from various branches of the ecumenical Christian community of which he is part. They have been chosen, though, for the professional and technical expertise which they bring to the table. For Nigel does not see Childnet International as some kind of Christian mission. Rather it should from the start clearly be established as a secular not-for-profit charity[3] able to work with a range of partners from industry, government and other NGOs both in the UK and abroad. So his trustees have to be plugged into to the mainstream. They include Mike Sheridan, tall laid-back Mike Conway, Mike Hastings, who would later be made a peer, and (just to prove that being named Mike was not a prerequisite to becoming a trustee) one of the Antioch leaders, Tom Bick.

"Picture the scene," Mike Conway would later write. "A friend of yours with a family and in a stable job tells you he has a vision to start up a new charity to help all those with the care for children respond to the emerging issues of the Internet. When you ask him has he got funding to start this new work, he tells you, NO. Premises? NO. Staff eager to help? NO. And how big should this venture be? 'International' is the reply."[4]

When the late Sam Wanamaker set out to build a replica of Shakespeare Globe on London's Bankside, a colleague commented wryly, "Working for Sam, you will have to prepare large quantities of ready-mixed concrete to support castles in air." Perhaps deep down some of Nigel's trustees felt the same way. They certainly needed to be men of faith as well as business acumen, for in the very early days, faith was Nigel's main asset – his passionate conviction that children and the Internet was a major issue, that now was the time to address it, and that he was the man for the job.

Naturally fundraising proved the dominant item on the agenda. Between them Nigel, Tom and the three Mikes drew up a list of potential donors. In early July Nigel sent out some twenty letters to individuals sharing the idea and asking them for help. At work, Lyndon and Charlie encouraged him with their generous response to his proposal. "Charlie's word to me was… 'Step out in faith'… 'Go for it'… 'CARE wants to support you 100%.'"[5] There followed weeks of waiting… hoping… praying and then, in a matter of days, money flowed in.

"What an unbelievable week, Lord. £50,000! Your provision," Nigel jubilantly comments.[6] (Pause for mental adjustment as the trustees suddenly realise they now have more than a notional role). The promised cash – the business equivalent, as one of his first employees would put it, to starting an international organisation with a pocket full of loose change – fell considerably short of the

£150,000 pump priming figure, never mind the £500,000 Nigel reckoned the venture needed. Still it was enough to equip an office and pay him a modest salary while he networked, came up with an action plan and sought funding for specific projects.

Again it is telling to recall how with the Computer Learning Centre, Nigel went for the big splash – state of the art premises, a major advertising campaign, a full complement of staff. In hindsight he reckoned he'd gone too far too fast. Experience taught him that it would be better for Childnet to start small. He established its first office in a partitioned-off section of the king-sized master bedroom in 14 Talfourd Road. He decided to employ no-one until he was sure their jobs would be secure. Indeed £20,000 of his funding package took the form of the salary he had been promised by an educational charity in return for several hours work a week for the next six months. So you could say that in those early days, Childnet International's only employee was a part-time CEO. A solo flute as opposed to a symphony orchestra. Enough, nonetheless, to raise the tune.

"Final day at CARE," he records on 31 August 1995. "Lovely farewell. Had the opportunity to speak and comment on the need to listen to God. Also told lots of funny stories." He kept a copy of his notes for that farewell speech – along with the cards and letters of appreciation which he received from friends and colleagues. Frustratingly the funny stories aren't fleshed out but, the notes do highlight what Nigel perceived to be the main fruits of his seven years of dedicated lobbying.

"We have achieved seven amendments to legislation and countless other changes to public policy. Premier Radio would not be broadcasting today without our work… And I believe perhaps the crowning glory – euthanasia would have been legalised without our work."

It is a sign of the times that in the latest formulation of the Human Fertilisation and Embryology Bill, his hard-fought-for amendment on a child's right to a father has been swept away. Premier Christian Radio[7] continues to broadcast though, and the political intern programme which Nigel helped get off the ground goes from strength to strength.[8] Nigel left his mark on CARE and carried away with him a wealth of experience and good relationships.

The entry in his diary next morning reads simply, "First day of the rest of my life."

NOTES

1) From 'An opportunity to help the children of the world – Responding to the Challenge of The Internet and Information Superhighway', 1995.

2) From 4 September (1985 journal).

3) Childnet's ethos and values were based on Nigel's personal Christian values. In time, as the organization grew and developed, staff were recruited and trustees appointed from a range of backgrounds and other experiences.

4) From Childnet International Annual Review 2002-03.

5) From Tuesday 11 July (1995 diary).

6) From Friday 21 July (1995 diary).

7) Owned by the charity Premier Christian Media Trust, Premier Christian Radio is a British Christian radio station broadcasting Christian programming to the London area. Premier can also be heard nationally on Sky, Virgin Media, and Freeview, and globally via its website.

8) This programme is now known as 'The Care Leadership Programme for Christian Graduates'.

CHAPTER FOURTEEN

JUGGLING

IN THE WEEKS THAT followed Nigel pressed ahead with realising his Childnet dream. He made appointments, set out a plan for the month, and came up with a draft itinerary for a trip to the USA. Travel, he knew, would be essential in establishing an international operation. But leaving CARE did not give him anything like the amount of time he really felt he needed to make things happen. If anything the tension between his paid employment and voluntary political work became even more marked. "Father, I feel nervous – apprehensive about the future and whether I have taken on too much" he wrote as 1995 drew to a close.[1]

Again, a Childnet Trustees' meeting in January highlighted his concerns that initial progress had been relatively slow. Still he continued to think big. In a blue folder amongst his papers I come across an unassuming A4 sheet, typed in April 1996. It sets out the Childnet International Project Programme for 1996-97. By the end of March 1997, the part-time CEO aspired to have six staff members undertaking a wide range of projects.[2] He includes a proposal to hold a video conference between the UK and US parliaments to discuss child safety on the Internet.

At the time video conferences were a rare and exotic marvel – the pink-plumed hoophoe of the technology world – and Nigel was operating out of a glorified broom-cupboard. Yet he believed he had the weapons to pull off this intergovernmental coup. His arsenal included a Washington-based colleague, Nuala Holowiki, with whom he had established a business relationship on that first trip to the USA; a range of sympathetic peers and MPs in

Westminster; and crucially a Childnet trustee, working for the telecommunications giant Cable and Wireless.

It fell to Mike Conway to make the initial approach to one of the company's technical engineers. "A mate of mine wants to set up a video conference discussion between some political big wigs in the American Senate and some of our folk here. It's to do with keeping children safe on the Internet. Could you... you know... help with the kit and communications and give him a hand?"

The engineer considered. "For children you say?"

Mike nodded with a typically disarming grin.

His colleague grinned back. "OK, then. I'll give it a try. But no promises, right?"

At this Nigel swung into action. There followed a flurry of emails, briefings, press releases, phone calls between Washington and London. The video conference was scheduled to take place on Wednesday 10 July – hosted by no less a person than the BBC's then Washington Correspondent Bridget Kendall.

One sleepless night and a day of "frantic last minute arrangements" later Nigel and his troops went over the top.

"Five radio interviews this morning... nerve-wracking waiting for the conference to start," he recorded, "BUT IT HAPPENED, and I think some good things came out of it."

"It was a prime example," Mike Conway observed later, "of something we saw over and over again in Childnet. A small organisation punching way above its weight."

A mere two weeks later though, this same valiant one-year-old organisation was on the ropes. At their monthly meeting in the Talfourd Road front room, the trustees looked grave. Laid out before them on the table were the Childnet accounts and the vital signs spelt 'crisis'. Childnet urgently needed financial life support. What to do? Nigel couldn't instantly move into resuscitation mode. The summer holidays had started. The next day the he and the family planned to head off to Germany with their close friends, the Alexanders and the Kyles. They would be out of the country for almost three weeks.

Alone, in the aftermath of that sober discussion, he recalled a hunkered weightlifter he'd seen on TV that morning "trying to snatch a huge weight." He'd watched the man wrap his fingers round a barbell, his body tense, his muscles bunched and straining. The feat had looked impossible. Yet incredibly the human tank had straightened, triumphantly lifting the load. The image spoke of victory. "The weight is on. Father, help me stand up," Nigel wrote.[3]

Then he set off for the Black Forest. He went, unsure whether his infant charity would still be a going concern when he came back. The weight of uncertainty was his barbell. Being with Louis and John and their families helped. Heather recalls Nigel sharing with them and receiving a great deal of encouragement. At the end of the first week he wrote… "A thoroughly enjoyable week. Good conversation. Lots of exercise – cycle rides at least once a day. Now as we start the second week I have questions… but not sure which is the key question…"[4]

That morning he set out his query stall. "Am I doing some activity which God would have me stop? Or am I spending too much time on something, or doing something in an ineffective way? Conversely should I be doing something I'm not already doing which would change life?"

The focus narrows, "Specifically have I got the emphasis right between money raising, Childnet and politics? How can I get further assistance? What sort of assistance do I need? Am I being inhibited by operating from home – does it induce false thinking?" He zooms in on his political activities, "Why am I in politics?

What does God want me to do in what manner? (conscious that how you do politics can be as important as what you do)…" And then in block capitals, indicative of the most pressing concern: "HOW DO I EARN/SECURE ENOUGH MONEY TO LET MY FAMILY SURVIVE?"

On this occasion, no single issue emerged as the hinge on which the door to clarity would swing open. Rather through the whole process Nigel found an inner release. "Father I thank you that these seem welcome questions," he concludes. "Because you are the God of answers – the God of leading us on and showing us your way, the God of security and of ideas and of fun…"

So for another week the fun continued. "Fruit picking with Elizabeth", "Lynda for an icecream", "Heather and I walked to the top of Hornisgrinde," "swimming pool in Fasbachwalden." Nigel relaxed, swam, cycled, went sightseeing.

Over the weekend of the 18 August, the family travelled via Paris back home to London. Home to good news. Miracle, coincidence, call it what you will, the fact remains that while they were away, several individuals put cheques into the post. Heather recollects the amazement and joy of finding those letters on the doormat. However you view it, the result was a lifeline – unexpected funding to the tune of over £16,000.

Despite this happy end to the financial crisis, it highlighted for Nigel the relentless challenge of juggling family, Childnet and politics. He really didn't have enough hours in the day or days in the week to do all the initiating that was required. He needed time to fundraise for Childnet, but how could he begrudge hours given to Council and committee meetings which had such a positive impact on people's lives?

By 1996 the programme to regenerate Peckham's five sink estates was steaming ahead.

We're going to fast forward here. In January 2007, Simon and I went walk-about in Peckham. (Simon, true gentleman that he is, shortening his long stride to match mine.) We strolled down Talfourd Road (pausing to pay our respects to No 14), past the fire station and the high rise flats. We made our way back round the corner to Peckham Road – stood on the steps of Southwark Town Hall, peered in though the glass of a locked front door, into the bureaucratic nerve-centre where his father had spent so many impassioned hours. Then we wandered through the Rye Lane shopping precinct. My impression all along was of an upbeat, vibrant community with a colourful dash of the Caribbean. Simon, though, kept muttering, "It's all so different… so different to the way it was…" Fresh in his mind were memories of unrenewed Peckham – a deprived, depressing, down-at-heel place.

The contrast between Peckham in 2007 and the Peckham Simon remembered flags up the difference made by the regeneration programme of the nineties. All through the early days of Childnet, Councillor Williams worked tirelessly in the community. "Nigel was always working to make sure Council was made to account for the way it moved forward with the renewal and in the way local interests were taken into account," Sarah Harrison would say. He also worked tirelessly in the Party. In April 1996 he had been asked to stand as Leader. Allowing his name to go forward as Deputy Leader instead, he was elected unopposed. Yet even the Deputy Leadership added significantly to his burdens.

And it didn't stop there. Just as in Enfield's film *Zulu*, every time the hapless British troops in Rorke's Drift fight off a wave of Zulu warriors, another horde appear on the horizon and come plunging down towards them, so January 1997 brought Nigel's political 'Zulu' experience. He was selected by the Lib Dems to fight for the Camberwell and Peckham seat in the forthcoming

General Election. Pitted against him: dapper conservative, Kim Humphries and the then Shadow Health secretary, Harriet Harman.

That spring electioneering took over Nigel's life. He prepared election literature, climbed stairs, knocked doors, leafleted, debated. For fifteen years a seat on the green benches of the Commons had been his goal. Many of those who knew him best and had the highest regard for his abilities, probably regarded this as unrealistic. He didn't view it that way. He had, after all, achieved every other step of his 1983 career plan. Of course common-sense stated he couldn't beat this particular sitting labour candidate in a safe labour seat. Officially he set his sights on second place. Privately, though, his ever irrepressible optimism may have whispered, "you never know!"

—m—

Folded into the front of Nigel's 1997 diary is a copy of an email. It isn't dated but appears to have been written soon after Tony Blair swept to power with his stunning 178 seat majority. All over Britain Labour won new seats and held onto old, including, unsurprisingly, Camberwell & Peckham. It reads as follows:

Dear Friends,

The result in Camberwell & Peckham was: Harriet Harman (Labour) 19,734, Kim Humphries (Conservative) 3,283, Nigel Williams (Lib Dem) 3,198.

We almost achieved our objective of second place, and certainly would have were it not for Mr Gerald Williams who was not seen in the constituency during the campaign, did not issue any election literature and did not even turn up at the count. My conservative opponent generously acknowledged that this was the case...

Immediate reflections are that we fought the good fight and learnt from the experience. Harriet met me in the street yesterday and said, "Nigel why don't you go and find a Tory seat to fight and win – you're too good a candidate to fight a battle here." I told her I was committed to the area and the people here and felt it was very important for democracy to hold Labour to account in the Inner City…

I live to fight another day – now to relax, pray and reflect on a most vital and illuminating experience…

Nigel's response to defeat echoes a philosophical nugget once viewed on the loop announcement system at a local railway station. There, nose to tail with the 'welcome to Belfast' and 'do not leave your baggage unattended' exhortations, the words padded round like a captive tiger circling his cage: "Experience is what you get when you don't get what you want."

It also demonstrates the strategies he had developed to off-set the negative emotions associated with failure – emotions succinctly summed up by three school children when asked how people feel about losing.

"Sad," said one.

"Sorry," said another.

"Humiliated," said a third with a gleeful grin.

Fortunately Nigel's innate self-belief inoculated him against humiliation. Failure did not make him defensive. His pragmatism gave little ground to regret. In this David and Goliath contest, Harman (a well-tailored Goliath in winter-white jacket and heels) had won. Nigel's reaction typified his response to every experience. He wanted to reflect – reflect and learn from it. He never shied from confronting negatives to extract a positive – some lesson that could refine his character and/or be carried away for future reference.

In this instance, however, musings on his 1997 election campaign were cut short. "I have to leave elections behind," he notes in early May.[5] For several months Childnet International had been starved of his attention. "Must make good progress in Childnet work today... I know I have been distracted..."[6] The fledgling charity is crying for his time – a cry which in the coming months would trigger the most difficult decision of his career.

NOTES

1) From Monday 18 December (1995 diary).
2) Some of the projects were research-based, some designed to promote good practice, others to educate and inform. The fourteen nascent ventures include "an evaluation of the effectiveness of 'blocking software' in preventing children gaining access to undesirable content" (this was to be a joint project with Professor Harold Thimbleby of Middlesex University), and an awards scheme for examples of good practice.
3) From Tuesday 30 July (1996 diary).
4) From Saturday 10 August (1996 diary).
5) From Friday 9 May (1997 diary).
6) From Monday 12 May (1997 diary).

CHAPTER FIFTEEN

WHEN A DREAM MUST DIE

THE SETTING IS A hotel on the Portobello Road. The date is 2 May – the day of Nigel's election defeat. He sits drinking coffee with American journalist, Larry Magid. Their conversation unfolds in the easy, animated manner that happens when two people with lots in common meet up. As a member of the board of directors for the National Centre for Missing and Exploited Children and founder of Safekids.com (one of the first websites to provide parents with advice) Magid could almost be Nigel's transatlantic doppelganger – right down to a mirror image moustache.

They are talking about the Childnet Awards – a scheme to reward children who make the most of the creative, educational and world citizenship opportunities the web provides.

"The launch site will invite entries from individuals," Nigel leans back in his chair. "But there'll be awards for schools and not-for-profit organisations too."

The warmth of Larry's response makes it easy for him to voice his request.

"I was rather hoping you'd be the main judge in the individual category?"

Without hesitation, Larry agrees. Better still, he offers his services on an expenses-only basis. Seeing him diarize the date of the autumn adjudication meeting reminds Nigel that he has under six months to get the whole project up and running – launched, funded, children and organisations encouraged to enter, entries shortlisted...

He experiences the familiar rush of excitement tinged with

panic at the thought. A lot hangs on the outcome of this venture. Indeed with his customary foresight he knows that this will be a make or break year for Childnet.

Despite frenetic activity, the site launch planned for early June has to be aborted. "Was to have been launch," his chastened note-to-self reads. "Relieved it didn't happen in the end, but considerable sense of personal failure in this… Election was the real bogey that threw things off course."[1]

True, the election may have thrown things of course, but this was far from the whole story. Throughout May Nigel's juggling act has continued, with a raft of council issues to attend to. On the Childnet front, funding applications, meetings with Internet Watch Foundation (the UK's hotline for reporting illegal content on the web) not to mention a small avalanche of arrangements to be made for a trip to Australia and the States, have all played their part in the delay.

One of the qualities that made Nigel a leader (as well as an entrepreneur) was his strategic foresight. "To live wisely," he notes. "You must be clear-sighted and realistic."[2] If a realistic course of action is one which takes account of prevailing circumstances and is alert to a full range of possible consequences (negative and positive), then Nigel operated realistically. He forged ahead – but never blindly.

In the autumn of 1997 most men would have described the Williams family-life as 'fine'. Heather and the children had accepted that Childnet business must constantly take Nigel away from home. Indeed there were benefits, as he brought a family member with him whenever he could. They didn't even object too much when the wanderer returned only to make a dozen phone-calls, sift through a mountain of Council paperwork and dash off to a committee meeting before unpacking. Still Nigel recognised, before anyone else ever said or saw it, that never mind the tension between Council and Childnet, his home-life was at risk.

"Father I desperately desire to follow you and I don't want to walk away from responsibility but I'm very concerned about family," he writes. "I do not want to get this wrong in a way that badly affects family." (3)

Again another man might have paid lip service to the problem and then continued merrily (or more likely wearily) on his way. But Nigel always went for solutions. His unblinkered assessment of the situation told him, simply and starkly, that he could not continue to juggle three balls. One must be relinquished. It could not be his family. It could not be Childnet. Therefore it must be his seat on Council.

So far, so good. To the uninvolved spectator, this looks like a no-brainer. Councillor Williams has served his local community tirelessly for the best part of four years. He will be leaving Peckham's five sink estates in infinitely better order than he found them. His contribution will be missed but the wheels of local government will continue to turn. Yet for Nigel the decision was far from simple. To the end of his days he would maintain that it was one of the hardest of his life.

The difficulty, in part, was spiritual. For fifteen years a sense of God's call to 'activate politically' had dominated his thinking and he had understood that call in terms of his ultimate election to parliament. Before he could move on, he had to let go of this ingrained understanding; accept a different interpretation of those words; believe they were being fulfilled in another way.

And there was emotional difficulty too. At gut level, one feels, Nigel would have echoed Willy Loman's comment in *Death of a Salesman,* that he aspired to "the greatest career a man could want." Alongside devotional volumes, for years the biographies/memoirs of politicians past and present – William Wilberforce, Gladstone, Dennis Healey, Paddy Ashdown (to make a random selection) – had formed his reading matter. Whenever he had taken a time out for reflection, 'politics' had been a significant heading in his life review. Now Nigel the realistic idealist had come up against his mid-life nemesis, Nigel the idealistic realist. It was not just a question of realising that God's will could be fulfilled in another sphere of work, it was accepting the stark word 'never'. To let go of his Council seat, was also to let go of the green benches of the Commons. It was to face the fact that he would never achieve that goal.

Another resolutely positive internationalist, the American political journalist Norman Cousins observed, "Death is not the greatest loss in life. The greatest loss is what dies inside us while we live." A dream died in Nigel that autumn – or rather a dream was put to death. He did not walk away from Southwark Council, he severed himself from it – first, mentally, as the hours of daylight shortened and the decision not to stand for re-election was made; then physically, when his term finally ended in May the following year.

NOTES
1) From Tuesday 3 June (1997 diary).
2) From Wednesday 11 March (1998 diary).
3) From Monday 20 October (1997 diary).

CHAPTER SIXTEEN

NEW GROWTH

THE SETTING IS THE Williams' Talfourd Road front room. The date, Wednesday 21 January – Nigel's forty-third birthday. Cards line the mantel-piece, the smell of the steak Heather is cooking for tea drifts mouth-wateringly from the kitchen. Nigel sits in an armchair with Jim, the dog, by his side, reading – no devouring – an article in *The Times*.

Whao! He punches the air. The vividly-written column comes from the pen of distinguished technical journalist Dorothy Walker – her chosen subject, the Childnet Awards.[1] Plainly Ms Walker applauds the scheme. She has attended the Awards Ceremony. She has interviewed Samantha, whose prize-winning school has helped her set up a chat line with two other girls, in Australia and America, and see them on a tiny TV screen. She has heard other young award-winners, from Australia, UK and Ireland, enthuse about the way the Internet has opened doors into new educational and cultural experiences.

The favourably impressed Ms Walker is just one of Childnet's many new fans, won over by the culmination to its three-day awards programme – a technical tour de force alive with the warmth of human personality. The BBC featured it in their flagship children's programme Blue Peter. Cable and Wireless, the scheme's major sponsor, have promised further funds. Would it have surprised these big players to learn that their glossy welcome packs had been put together by a family team in the back of a bedroom? Possibly not. For in his long reach from a lowly base, Nigel incarnates the spirit of the dot-com revolution – a lone individual in a box room with a computer and a modem heading up a global nerve centre.

Now every postal delivery, it seems, brings letters of congratulation. Childnet supporters express their delight. Competition winners express their gratitude. For judge Larry Magid one of the high points has been "watching winners from a school in Indiana and another in the Netherlands meet for the first time after collaborating on a joint project regarding endangered animals throughout the world."

One of the things which gives Nigel the most pleasure is his sense of the ripple effect. The Micklefield school in South Africa came first in the Schools category. They tell him they plan to use their prize money to buy a new computer for one of the poorest schools in their area. A wheelchair-bound sixteen-year-old came first in the individual category. He says he has been encouraged to continue with his computer studies and plans to donate part of his prize money to the Musclar Distrophy Association of Queensland.

"Father, I thank you for the amazing and moving triumph that was the awards ceremony," Nigel notes. "None of us anticipated that it would turn out quite as 'charged' as it was. A real <u>frisson</u> of excitement... Lord, help us not to sink as a result of this but to fly and soar and do your will in the way you want us to!"[2]

The setting is an empty glass-fronted office looking out on a corrugated-iron walkway. The date is 9 March 1998. For several minutes Nigel stands in the centre of the room, contemplating the light, echoing space, conjuring up mental pictures of desks in corners and filing cabinets against walls. Then with a proprietorial air, he exits, locking the door behind him as he goes.

That evening he pens a jubilant scribble, "Lunch with Steve C D.

He accepted the job! – unit at Brockley 14 – excitement!!"
Interpreted, this means that within the space of twelve hours
Childnet has acquired another full-time member of staff and office
premises in a business centre in South London.

For some employees the idea of building your desk before you
can sit at it would be off-putting. Not so for Stephen Carrick-
Davies. The new staff member relishes the thought of a fresh
canvas. This, in part, is what has enticed him away from his
position as director of another charity to work with Nigel. "It
was the seemingly impossible, almost outrageous vision that Nigel
had for Childnet, as much as the opportunity to be in at the start
and make a positive contribution to the Internet revolution that
attracted me," he recalls. "It was radical at that time to involve
young people in the delivery of services, challenging to want to
work internationally, and refreshing that Nigel had such faith in
people's potential and ability."[3] Stephen shared Nigel's excitement
in stepping into the blank industrial unit that was to become the
new Childnet offices – in putting together the flat pack furniture.
It was the excitement of pioneering something new.

Over the next two years the charity surges ahead. Highly
successful awards ceremonies take place in Sydney and in Barbados.
For the Barbados awards an international panel of judges, of which
Larry Magid remains a key member, must choose between entries
from 25 countries across every continent. Winners include website
projects from Australia, Canada, Costa Rica, India, Ireland,
Namibia, Romania, the UK and the USA.

"What has been wonderful this year is to see how people with
limited resources, living in countries with limited Internet usage,
are developing outstanding innovative projects that are world class,"

Nigel comments. "In addition, many of the winning projects this year dramatically show how children who are at risk of illness or homelessness can use the Internet to highlight their situation and challenge others to respond."[4]

Anyone with any awareness of Nigel's longstanding concern for the poor and disadvantaged in society would realise that these were much more than politically correct words. Promoting Internet access to children and young people worldwide was what Childnet (in part) was about.

At the same time the need to keep children safe provided an equally strong driving force. Here too the charity had been playing a strategic role. The photograph on the back of the annual review for 1998-99 shows a staff team which had mushroomed from two to seven. It includes Nigel's long standing friend Louis Alexander in the role of 'hotline consultant'.

"A hotline," as Nigel explained to supporters, "is a means by which users who come across illegal items on the Internet can report these to the hotline which then takes action either by asking the Service Provider to remove the item or informing the police."[5]

Hotlines, in other words, help in the fight against child pornography, but for the campaign to be effective, global cooperation is required. And before agencies (especially agencies with different policies, legal constraints and funding procedures, made up of people from different cultures and backgrounds) can cooperate, they need to come together and develop common procedures. "Meeting these requirements," as the cobbler said to the centipede, "is a challenge!" It takes effort, patience, commitment – above all it takes skilled leadership.

Enter Childnet in the person of Nigel Williams – Coordinating Prime Mover extraordinaire! Over the years, at CARE and on

Southwark Council, he had proved that one of his great skills lay in getting people from diverse backgrounds to pursue common goals. It was Nigel who initially obtained funding to bring together a small group of hotline providers from ten European countries – the group which was to become the INHOPE forum. He subsequently helped them agree and develop their statutes, chaired the meeting where they voted to become a registered association and generally assisted in the whole area of policy development.

The setting is the Channel 4 newsroom. The date is 24 October 2000. Nigel sees his face in the monitor and knows that he is about to appear live in hundreds of thousands of homes across the land. Today Patrick Green – the first paedophile to be convicted of using an online relationship to groom a young person and lure her into having sex – has been sentenced. For parents all over the country, his trial has been a major wake-up call. But Nigel got there first.

At seven o'clock in the evening, as anxiety levels peak, his voice comes over the airwaves – deliberate, measured, reassuring. Never one for the empty sound-bite, he directs listeners and viewers to the newly launched Childnet site www.chatdanger.com. Stephen has written the content. A number of experts from the UK and around the world have reviewed what he's said. It provides a clear, balanced safety message, emphasising that online chat in itself is neither wrong nor dangerous. Stephen has included advice on how to evaluate a good chat room as well as advice on how chat can be constructively used.

For his part Nigel goes on to do around thirty media interviews over the course of the next 72 hours – at the end of which Childnet receives a note from the British TV newscaster Martyn Lewis CBE. "I simply had to drop you a note to congratulate you on the simply fantastic coverage for "chatdanger"... an absolute classic of its kind, which should go down in charity case-histories as the best way to enhance the profile and address a real publicly perceived need at the same time."

But the story does not end there. Childnet has not only developed a timely website; every bit as important in Nigel and Stephen's eyes, they have supported Patrick Greene's victim and her family. Moreover they have written to eight leading providers of chat services to suggest a number of ways in which they could improve safety. Will Gardner, their research officer, has been collaborating with another expert to prepare a paper on UK law reform and they had been in touch with the victim's MP.

In the months which follow the Chatdanger site receives over 800 emails from children asking for advice. Nigel, meanwhile, is invited to join the Home Office Taskforce on Children Protection, established partly in response to their lobbying. This group in turn refines and builds on a Childnet proposal to criminalise grooming which is adopted by the then Home Secretary, David Blunkett.

For Nigel and Stephen the whole sequence of events embodies Childnet's approach. They are about people – networking, relating, supporting, encouraging, bringing together; they are about programmes – creating, developing, celebrating positive innovation; and they are about policy – researching, highlighting, warning, lobbying and liaising with those who can bring about change. Again, for them both, why and how they do these things are as vital as what they do. Their ethos is one of Christian service – not-for-profit, unconditional, simply setting out to achieve the greatest, most inclusive, international common good.

The setting is a park. The date, 2 January 2001. These days

visitors to Peckham Rye park will find gardens and walkways, arguably as lovely as ever they were in their elegant Victorian prime. But on the cold winter morning in question that restoration has yet to take place. Nigel strides along a path that was once an elm-lined avenue, past a silted pond that was once a lake, through a confusion of weeds and ferns and grasses. The park is a bit like middle age. It may not be anything like as beautiful as it once was. It may not be as treasured as it will become. Still it is an excellent place to contemplate the future.

Nigel has set the day aside for reflection and planning. He knows the months ahead will be critical in terms of choices and decisions. Heather faces job uncertainty; the children are spreading their wings. Simon has followed in his father's footsteps to Cambridge; Lynda is keen to study art; Elizabeth is fascinated by all things neurological. Kathryn, now in her third year of medical studies, has a serious boyfriend. Is there an engagement in the offing? Still, on this walk, the future Nigel most wants to reflect on is that of Childnet.

As far as can ever be said of any small, not-for-profit organisation in an era of capricious core funding, the next few years seem secure. Childnet is now established. There is much to be thankful for… much to build on. Yet somehow, that morning Nigel finds himself distracted from planning for the charity's ongoing development. He feels the need to dig deeper.

And so he digs – beneath the successes, beneath the concerns, beneath the project ideas. A brave winter bird raises a song and suddenly his mental spade hits against something solid. A treasure? A grenade? One way or another it will need careful handling. For in this neglected place, he has unearthed a radical question. Could God be asking him to give Childnet away?

Back home in the reclaimed bedroom space of his erstwhile

office he examines his find. It is as intriguing as the bright cutting from some tropical plant. "I realise there is an important difference between being prepared to give Childnet away and preparing to give Childnet away," he muses. "I should definitely have the attitude, but perhaps God is calling me to the action. I ask why?"

Three possible reasons follow, two of which suggest that Nigel feels this would benefit Childnet – allowing the charity, in a sense, to take on an independent life. The third reason, which he is at pains to underscore as the <u>least</u> important is that it would release him "to other possibilities".

Reading between the lines one detects the first faint heady scent of a call to fresh adventure – sap rising to the stump from which 'politics' once branched.

NOTES
1) 'Live wires make the fur fly', *The Times*, Wednesday January 21, 1998.
2) From Monday 19 January (1998 diary).
3) Stephen would work for Childnet for over 10 years and succeeded Nigel as CEO in 2003.
4) From Childnet News (summer 1998).
5) Ibid.

CHAPTER SEVENTEEN

YEAR OF THE GARDEN

MID-AFTERNOON ON THE first Friday in February the telephone rings. Unusually Nigel is at home. With Heather away in Ireland for the week, he has left work early to be with Elizabeth. He lifts the receiver.

"Oh hi, there, Pete. How are things?" The genuine warmth of his greeting masks a faint pang. Medical student, Peter Yeates is an intelligent, thoughtful and caring young man. He is also astute enough to recognise a paragon of female perfection when he finds one. All of which leads the Nigel to suspect that this could be more than a casual call.

"I was wondering… I mean… I really want to marry Kathryn," says Pete. "If that's all right with you?"

"What a hard question to answer," Nigel wrote that night. His natural response certainly did not fit neatly under the monochrome 'all right' heading. How could giving a beloved eldest daughter away be 'all right' with any father worth his salt? The prospect was breath-taking… seismic… scary… "But very exciting."

This story-line apart, excitement kept a low profile over the next ten months. The year 2001 could be described as a period of routine ups and downs, during which Nigel devoted chunks of time to the garden. His diary records Saturdays spent brushing up leaves, fencing, planting, filling in a pond and digging out the roots of old trees stumps. There are also a number of entries in which he refers to a general loss of drive.

"I am in one of those funny lackadaisical periods where I am getting things done but not incisively… I know this experience is one I have had on many occasions throughout my life… I confess my weakness. I desire to overcome it and move forward"[1], he had noted mid-January.

Two weeks passed but the lack of motivation didn't. "Woke up feeling pretty wretched," reads his diary entry for 30 January. "Decided… to go and see Louis today. Tell him about my detachedness."

As a result of this conversation Nigel determines to pray and fast on Tuesdays and to get an exercise routine going. Wise friend that he is, Louis also counsels him to pick up on things that had gone well and not to be too hard on himself. But it is not until the beginning of March, after a trip to Singapore, that Nigel says he has at last been "knocked out of my slumber and post Xmas depression."[2] Clearly the burst of vigour doesn't last. In early May he records a significant chat with Heather about drifting. "We both sense that we have been in a state of real drift on a range of issues and need to get a much better handle on things."[3] Once again he resolves to do better, only this time his good intentions are overridden by physical sickness, which also seems to be a recurrent feature of these months.

The year culminates (diary-wise) in dozens of blank pages followed by a telling Christmas Eve entry.

"A couple of months have gone by without making any entries at all in this journal," he notes. "Symptomatic of my allowing life to wash over me this year. It's strange – I've done more practically at home, especially in the garden, this year than for a long time. But this has perhaps been an escape – something to do that is pre-set – a mountain to climb simply because it is there. I feel like I've drifted generally in the right direction but without sharpness…"

And on that note, with a few further desultory references to food, the weather and Kathryn's forthcoming marriage, the year of the garden comes to an end.

NOTES
1) From Wednesday 17 January (2001 diary).
2) From Monday 5 March (2001 diary).
3) From Monday 7 May (2001 diary).

CHAPTER EIGHTEEN

SABBATICAL

AND NOW IT'S SPRING. The setting is All Saints Church, Peckham. Within its granite walls fresh flowers waft their scent and the gentle hum of conversation fills the air. At 2.00 pm precisely there's a rustle of silk; a turning of heads; an expectant hush. The heraldic harmonies of Pachelbel's Canon ring out and the bride, radiant in white, makes her entrance on her father's arm. It's 2 March 2002. Happy, proud, savouring the drama of the moment, Nigel walks Kathryn down the aisle.

"Who gives this woman to be married to this man?"

"I do."

He steps back into the pew beside Heather and together they hear their eldest daughter and her fiancé make their vows. "For better, for worse, for richer, for poorer, in sickness and in health..." The young couple speak with clarity and deep commitment.

"You may kiss the bride."

Cue for loud cheers and clapping. The same blend of tradition mixed with warm-hearted spontaneity and freedom to be different which had characterised Nigel and Heather's own wedding twenty-four years earlier is present today. Lights flash and cameras click as the wedding party leaves the building. Then, taxis waved off, the guests pile into the red London bus that will ferry them over to the reception in Greenwich.

"Wonderful... fantastic... a thrill," are words Nigel uses to describe the experience. But it brings a tear in the eye too. This is a major transition after all – a daughter finally gone from the family nest. His steady, beautiful, brilliant Kathryn beginning a new life with her Peter. It is a watershed moment in any parent's book. There is sadness also that Heather's sister Angela, still in a coma, cannot be with them and that Idwal, standing alongside Sheila and Sue, with her husband David, does not have Rene by his side. Her death, ten years previously, has been the first break in the Williams family circle. Still she had lived long enough to enjoy her grandchildren and to make a new home in the historic mill town of Buckfastleigh where, at the age of 69, Idwal had been appointed lay pastor. Now Grandad Williams' inimitable rendering of grace before the meal proves one of the highlights of the reception.

On Saturday – champagne and wedding cake. On Monday morning – back to porridge. Routine days in the Childnet offices come interspersed with routine travel – a conference in Hong-Kong, a mid-month trip to Cambodia and a stint setting up the Childnet Awards in Paris. Some routine, you might say. But. routine, like beauty, is in the eye of the beholder and having spent six years in the fast-lane, Nigel has entered his seventh at the wheel. As we have seen, throughout the preceding year he has felt that he has taken his foot off the accelerator.

"Time for a sabbatical," the Childnet Trustees agree.

—◠—

A sabbatical (from the Greek sabbatikos) is a prolonged hiatus, typically one year, in the career of an individual taken in order to fulfil some goal. Never an adherent of the typical, Nigel decided on an abridged version following on from the family summer holiday. His goal would be to expand his intellectual, cultural and spiritual horizons. He and his trustees saw it as two months – July and August – of refuelling.

In early May, amid the general push to ensure that programmes and projects would run smoothly in his absence, he took a day out to pray and to reflect.

"Really want to have a blank sheet of paper so will start by worshipping God and seeking clarity on the right questions," he notes at the outset.

By early afternoon he is ready to get down to specifics. He seeks "a picture of the next steps" and what springs to mind is an image of expansion. Taken in context it would appear to represent a vision for Childnet, with the echo of a direction for his own life. It is "of moving from a garden with some successful plants to a well-organised farm…"[1]

———

Two months later Nigel motored through the gates, not of a well-organised farm, but of a well-organised agricultural college in Northern Ireland. Greenmount College, with its fertile acres and magnificently restored ornamental gardens, had once been a fine gentleman's desmesne. The newly arrived delegate made his way up between ionic columns into the vaulted entrance hall of the magnificent sandstone Manor House.

"Well, look who's here! Great to see you again…" a familiar voice rang out.

Nigel grinned. The figure coming towards him, hand outstretched, was his old Portadown friend, Derek Poole, now working as a programme director for ECONI[2], the group responsible for the conference he had come to attend. Billed as a summer school on a 'spirituality for social engagement', this was a gathering for Christians engaged professionally in the secular world. It was aimed at busy practitioners. All very relevant to Nigel.

Very quickly he realised he could let down his defences. "Beautiful surroundings… peacefulness, a haven, an important institution for Ulster's farming community," he records. "Felt very welcomed… Derek got sharing going. He has a delightful and deep knowledge of all sorts of things… a man at peace with himself…"[3]

The important word here is 'sharing'. The summer school was not structured round key-note speeches and seminars. It was a time to reflect, to share and to make inner journeys. The programme included experimenting with movement, listening to music, journaling, exploring new ways of listening to God through Scripture, and praying the Scriptures. Then came a module on 'the spirituality of letting go.' Faced with a group of influential individuals, each highly regarded in their own secular sphere, Derek gently challenged them to confront hidden hurts with a series of questions. What had pained them? Disappointed them? Caused them to be disappointed in their vocation? Had they grieved those losses? Had they been able to let them go?

That afternoon he and Nigel took a stroll round Greenmount's famed walled garden, with it aromatic geometrical patterns and intricate maze. It was the perfect opportunity for Nigel to talk through the loss of his political role.

"I remember saying that I was glad he hadn't become an elected politician," Derek recalls. "For two reasons: First, he would have had to surrender his visionary ideas for political pragmatism. For some people this is the right thing to do – but it wouldn't have been for him. Second, I felt he had a prophetic quality which is always more effective from the margins. He could say hard, honest things from the margins which he would not have been able to say from the centre."

Derek's perspective is worth considering. It is true that Nigel was an ideas person. It is true that his natural inclination was to function politically as an independent, and that he could make more happen, more quickly from the edge. Still his journals suggest that he did not view political pragmatism in terms of surrender. All the indications are that he found considerable fulfilment in his years as a Liberal Democrat counsellor. He had not chaffed against the party political game. He had played it – and played it with integrity, rising above personalities and infighting.

And yes, this had involved compromise. Nigel had always accepted that party politics came with a policy package. "In moving forward on the question of party political allegiance I consider that the first step is to define from the outset the important issues on which I am unwilling to compromise, and the other policies I would personally hold to on which compromise is possible," he had written in 1983. He went on to express his desire "to be honest, open and hardworking, sticking to my guns on crucial issues and negotiating a practical stance on others."[4]

One occasion when he had felt compelled to stick to those guns had occurred at the Liberal Democrat Party conference in 1994 – the year before he started Childnet. The issue, in this case, had been a paragraph in a policy document on economic sustainability which said, "adequate safe confidential family planning advice and services should be available to every UK citizen from puberty onwards."

The week before the conference Kathryn, then fourteen, had heard a radio report to the effect that the Liberal democrats supported the availability of contraception to 11 year olds. She was shocked. "If you set a law for people to consent to sexual relationships at sixteen, providing the Pill for them under that age is just stupid." She urged Nigel to speak out against the proposal – which he duly did.

"And the balloon went up," he comments wryly in his diary.[5] The media had a field day. "Mr Williams was the only delegate at the Brighton Conference to oppose the plan from the rostrum," trumpeted the Daily Mail. "Mr Williams demanded that the man behind the policy… should clarify the role of parents under the scheme… The MP is already under fire from the party leadership for saying too much about the policy and attracting unfavourable publicity."[6] One can imagine that Paddy Ashdown, the then leader of the Liberal Democrats, was none too pleased with Nigel either. This is one indication that had he become a backbencher in a Lib Dem government (admittedly an unlikely scenario), if pushed, he would have chosen to be branded a 'maverick' rather than toe the party line.

Eight years later, all this was history. What mattered now was moving on in the present. The ECONI conference allowed Nigel to lay questions to rest through sharing with an insightful friend. Further encouragement lay ahead. On the third day of the conference, after a trip to Nendrum monastry, Derek invited the group to consider the aesthetic, artistic dimension to their lives. He spoke to them about poetry: what it was, how to read it and – most challengingly – how to write a poem.

"Poetry will distil life down for you. Help you untangle complicated ideas," he explained. "The words, images and metaphors you choose will say something unique and distinctive about who you are. Get the first line and trust the process…"

Ready to give it a go, Nigel set off dutifully clutching his notebook. Half an hour later he was back, a 'eureka' sparkle in his eyes. Derek had been absolutely right. The words had come. The poem – his first ever – had taken shape.

"Just magic," he wrote of the poetry evening which followed. Bravely he'd shared his poem, had it critiqued, and been exhilarated by the whole experience. "No idea I could enjoy it so much… I'm feeling rich and full."[7]

—◆—

It could be argued that poetry provided a high octane boost to Nigel's emotional refuelling. He had always enjoyed wordplay, happily filling unclaimed moments with crosswords and games of scrabble. That summer in the face of philistine family teasing ("Dad, you've *really* lost it!"), he took to literary activity of a different order – mysterious, absorbing, deeply satisfying – a fresh way of marshalling thoughts, revealing himself to himself and others.

Over the summer months Nigel wrote twenty-six poems in all, each one immaculately typed up and dated. A number were written in art galleries and are accompanied by photographs of paintings they describe (Matisse's *Bowl of Oranges,* Picasso's *Figures at the Seashore,* Constable's *Hay Wain).* Others have a domestic theme. Many are based on Bible verses or on the experience of Bible characters: Pontius Pilate – the civil servant; Justus – the also-ran apostle; Joseph of Arimathea – the secret disciple; Ananias and Sophia – two early Christians who paid with their lives for an apparently small act of deception. All are characterised by close observation, directness, ethical and spiritual vision and human understanding. There is throughout an undercurrent of personal feeling and experience, although the word 'I' is never used. Perhaps, though, the most significant piece in the folder is not about elections or public life or hypocrisy, but a poem about dreams.

A clergy friend of mine maintains that sabbaticals are dangerous. To prove it he refers to erstwhile pillars of society who are granted sabbaticals, and next thing they've kicked over the traces and abandoned the grindstone for good. Perhaps the truth is that sabbaticals are not so much dangerous as unsettling. The unaccustomed change of pace gives space to uncover dreams mislaid under the layers of routine activity. They are times when yearnings surface.

"Your old men shall dream dreams. Important that as we get older we don't stop dreaming dreams!" Nigel notes mid-sabbatical in his diary. "Tandems, motor homes maybe, but even more changed lives, fulfilled hearts, values implemented… Father, may I not stop dreaming."[8] Here, it seems, he hits on the crux of what had been happening over the past eighteen months. His political quest had been his big dream and letting it go had de-energised him. Now a fresh recognition of the importance of big dreams comes through in a poem he wrote the same day, based on the same verse from the book of Acts.[9]

Old Men's Dreams

Dreaming is ageless
Performance doesn't falter as the body creaks.
Old men's dreams aren't wiser or more constrained
But age may stunt the dreamer's hope
Of seeing his fantasy realised

Edwards dreamed of a golden set.
Older than most the sand was slipping through,
But he focussed on the chance
That Manchester bought and
Hopped, skipped and jumped to fulfil the dream.

Our dreams may focus on increased leisure.
Children growing up, fewer ties that bind
We think of tandems, motor homes
Theatre nights, travel to islands in the sun.
But are these the dreams the prophet meant?

Yes, fantasies of fun and fulfilment
Lives replete in joy, enriched by friends.
But dreams also of wider impact
For cities, nations, peoples left behind
Dreams of justice, mercy and peace.

Our dreams can be realised
They need not linger in the sleepy bed.
People can be changed,
Lives healed from society's ills
If we but trust, His kingdom will come.

That September Nigel returned to his desk, hungry once again to dream big dreams and translate them into action. Autumn 2002 saw him throw himself into planning a major conference in Tokyo designed to explore the implications of the latest mobile phone technology in terms of Child Protection. "I sense I've been wandering a bit in the last 2-3 years," he writes as the year wears to a close. "Now I want to make God's impact again. Need to hear, need to be passionate… John Adams, that amazing American, [10] had periods of ineffectiveness and then fundamental decisiveness. I need the same… not for my own sake – but for others." [11]

NOTES

1) From Wednesday 8 May (2002 diary).
2) The summer school was run by ECONI (Evangelical Contribution on Northern Ireland) – a group set up under the directorship of David Porter to address community division in Northern Ireland and the long-term task of peace-building. Since 2005 it has been known as the Centre for Contemporary Christianity in Ireland.
3) From Wednesday 10 July (2002 diary).

4) From 'A Political Career', 27 July 1983.

5) From Thursday 22 September (1994 diary).

6) The flurry of press coverage included articles in the *Daily Express* and the *Daily Mail* and a number of other publications. *The Mail* article appeared on 23 September 1994 – headlined 'Kathryn, 14 says: You're being stupid over the Pill' (byline Sean Rayment).

7) From Friday 12 July (2002 diary).

8) From Monday 29 July (2002 diary).

9) Acts 2:17.

10) John Adams was the second President of the USA.

11) From Wednesday 4 December (2002 diary).

CHAPTER NINETEEN

DREAM JOB

THE FIRST GLIMPSE OF a fresh shore comes out of the blue one normal, busy but otherwise unremarkable day at the office. It's been a day spent selecting winners for the 2003 Childnet Awards – a choice between 270 entries from 50 countries. Fortunately Nigel has had the input of a lively, savvy youth panel to complement that of his distinguished nine-person adult team. Their new judges included TV presenter Carole Vorderman and associate editor of the Times Educational Supplement, Judith Judd, working alongside old hands such as Trond Waage, the Ombudsman for Children in Norway.

"Brilliant, isn't it – how both panels' verdicts have dovetailed," he said to Trond after a very satisfactory shortlisting meeting.

"That's teenagers for you," his companion grinned. Trond went on to throw an interesting aside into the conversation. A position similar to his own, but with even greater powers, was coming up in Northern Ireland. "I hear the Stormont Assembly may appoint a Commissioner for Children and Young People next spring. Would you be interested in such a post?"

Nigel considered. A post protecting the rights of children and young people? His pulse rate quickened. "Yes." Pause. "I might."

From that day on the thought lodged in his mind. By early January he had read through the new legislation passed to underpin the job – legislation rooted in the 1998 Belfast Agreement with its vision "of a peaceful, inclusive, prosperous, stable and fair society founded on the achievement of reconciliation, tolerance and mutual trust and the protection and vindication of human rights for all."

The statutes Nigel scanned so eagerly that January reflected the priority to be given to children and young people. Here were clauses signalling, amongst other things, an obligation on all governmental and non-governmental bodies to take account of their needs. The Children's Commissioner would be an independent political and social voice – a sworn enemy of those who sought to harm children and a critical friend to everyone else – free to initiate research, commission reports and monitor responses. Would Nigel be interested? "Ah let me at it," was his gut response.

A diary entry a couple of weeks later shows how the prospect had hooked him. "The biggest challenge is the Children's Commissioner job... I have felt a frisson – not sure if it is pride, ambition, calling but it has certainly been absorbing. H(eather) too has been very consumed by the thought and quite attracted to moving. We are finding it hard not to think about this..."[1]

In hindsight, two earlier diary entries also seem significant. One dates back to 4 June 2000 and refers to a church prayer-time after which a friend had taken Nigel to one side to predict that he would have the opportunity "to influence nationally, speaking for those who had no voice of their own."

"I cried." Nigel notes. "Don't know what it means but I know God is speaking."

The second entry, just over a year later, followed from his reading of the biography of Northern Ireland's then First Minister, David Trimble. Nigel noted that the book had "added interest" because of his son Simon's friendship with Trimble's son, Richard. "But also because I want to get under the skin of where NI is now and to see what place there might be for me."[2]

This throw-away comment hints at the constitutional marvel that had been unfolding for more than a decade on the other side of the Irish Sea. In 1988, the very year that the Williams had moved to England, John Hume had entered into secret discussions with Sinn Fein/IRA leader Gerry Adams. Against a backdrop of ongoing violence, dialogue, designed to wean paramilitaries away from bomb and bullet and build confidence in political solutions, stumbled out into the open. Ceasefires followed. Next came the watershed of the 1998 Belfast Agreement[3], then the 'pinch-me-I-must-be-dreaming' spectacle of Ulster Unionist David Trimble being sworn in as First Minister and nationalist Seamus Mallon as Deputy First Minister in a power-sharing Assembly.

Of course there had been and continued to be major set-backs along the way. At local level certain provisions of the Agreement caused bitter hurt and resentment; in the paramilitary ghettos intimidation and punishment beatings continued. Politically the Peace Process was frequently bogged down in a mire of distrust. Indeed in July 2001, shortly before Nigel made Trimble's biography his bedtime reading, the First Minister had resigned over a perceived lack of IRA decommissioning and the Assembly had been suspended. Again, in October 2002, some months before Nigel first heard of the Children's Commissioner's job, devolution was suspended following a complete break-down in confidence on the unionist side. Nevertheless the Province he now contemplated was a different world to the one he had left behind. The actual words 'the war is over' might not have been spoken – but that was the way it felt.

Nigel's diary entry reflects this new political and social landscape. It also flags up the fact that although, years previously his centre of gravity had shifted to England (with his parents, Sheila and

Sue following suit) the emotional pull towards Northern Ireland held firm.

In April 2003, as PM Tony Blair and Taoiseach Bertie Ahern pulled out all the political stops to haul the Peace Process out of the quagmire, a sheaf of pages headed 'Application for the Post of Commissioner for Children and Young People for Northern Ireland' appeared on Nigel's desk. Ten essential criteria. Four desirable criteria. Fourteen chunks of pristine white space waiting for his response. From the moment he set eyes on it, he too pulled out all the stops. For several days those dozen or so half-page boxes absorbed him. With Heather's full support, he drafted, discussed, redrafted, changed a sentence here, threw in a relevant illustration there and then substituted it for an even stronger one. Happily, this was not one of those exercises where collecting the tea money becomes 'valuable experience of budget management and stock control'. As he honed each pitch, it was with a sense of the unforced match between what he'd done to date as a civil servant, entrepreneur, political lobbyist, local councillor, school governor, managing director, children's advocate, and father, and what the post required.

—⁓—

Cut to a well-appointed room in a hotel conference suite. It's Monday 12 May 2003. During the preceding weeks in the corridors of power the political manoeuvring to reactivate the Assembly has continued and in the office of the First and Deputy First Minister Nigel has been short-listed for his dream job. Today he has two interviews. This first one will be conducted by young people and take the form of a videoed role-play.

Expectantly five young people size him up. For the next half hour, four of them will pretend to be members of a cross-community youth group. Nigel's task – to deliver a short talk on Children's Rights. What he hasn't been told is that each teenager has a fictitious life-issue due to impact in a major way on how they behave. In other words, this anodyne room with its kohl-eyed occupants is an artificial minefield, with four young people primed to blow up in his face.

"Nice to meet you," Nigel greets them easily.

They shift in their seats, waiting for his next move. Will he attempt to crack a joke? Write on the flipchart? Expound brightly?

No, instead of launching into a spiel on Children's Rights, Nigel simply sits himself down and smiles. "OK then. Tell me about yourselves..."

Afterwards he reckoned that this instinctive response saved him. As soon as the group start talking, the landmines surface. "I weaseled out of them what the issues were that were concerning them and the bitterness that there was between a couple of them," he would recall. "So all of this came out quite quickly." He was then able to explain in a natural way the relevance of children's rights to their individual situations and the conversation flowed.

As much as anything, this interview and the more conventional one which followed (again with a panel of young people), increased his enthusiasm for the job. Never mind the impression he had created, the panellists impressed him hugely. "Enjoyed yesterday's interviews with young people very much," he wrote early next morning. "It encouraged me. Made me think there can be a fresh start..."[4]

He returns to the Stormont Hotel that day for a further hour-long interview, this time with a mixed panel of adults and young people. The session begins with his own eight minute presentation on 'the challenges facing the Commissioner for Children and Young

People and how you would deal with them in your first twelve months in office.' Once again Nigel majors on the importance of listening. No doubt many voices will seek to gain the Children's Commissioner's ear, he surmises – politicians, civil servants, the media, voluntary groups, service providers. Each will have their agenda and important things to say. But first and foremost he must listen to children and young people. If he is offered the sun, moon and stars he can only take action when it is in their best interests. Their needs will be his top priority.

Nigel's Diary Thursday 5 June

Heard today, after three weeks of anguished waiting that I had got the NICCYP job! Whao! Blown away really! Can't quite take it in.

On the big screen, this would be the moment the camera pans out on the mystic vistas of happily-ever-after and the credits roll. The long months of not knowing have given Nigel space to examine his motives. "This has to be a service to God not a Nigel thing, a mission not a career move, a humble 'why send me' rather than 'please, sir, I can do it!'"[5] he has noted. But now he knows that there is indeed a place for him in the new Northern Ireland, a place where he will have the "opportunity to influence nationally, speaking for those who have no voice of their own." His career has come full circle, allowing this exile to return home, with real powers and a budget of £2 million to promote and protect the rights of children. The bright June morning is pregnant with a sense of denouement. He has achieved his dream of a political role.

In prime position, at the front of a ring-binder, a photocopy of his Children's Commissioner's job application has been filed, It seems no coincidence that stashed away at the back of this same folder is the yellowed type-script, entitled 'A Political Career', penned twenty years before. Between these two documents lie two decades of life in all its rich, messy, mundane, frustrating, exhilarating, pressurised, tragic and joyful variety; two decades of choices and decision-making; two decades of action and reflection. The document at the back of the file is largely aspirational, while the one at the front gives a snapshot of how it's all worked out – in Nigel's life as an individual and in the province to which he now knows he will return.

Setting these two documents side by side, one is reminded of singers starting a piece with musical accompaniment, continuing unaccompanied for several verses, and being rejoined by the piano – a nerve-wracking moment (especially for the conductor) which reveals if they've gone flat. These documents reveal that all through the 'unaccompanied' years, Nigel held his pitch. It's almost uncanny to see the extent to which by June 2003, he has achieved his personal and political goals. Despite the many demands of paid and unpaid employment, his family has not played second fiddle to his career. He has not been elected to parliament – but, bearing in mind Derek Poole's insights of the previous year, his new position offers him an edgier, more independent political role.

These intervening years have seen the budding of a new constitution full of power-sharing checks and balances in Northern Ireland. They have also seen many checks and balances to the power of the UK government as a whole. Politicians and ministers are now more readily held to account for their actions and decisions. The checks have come about partly as a result of engagement with the institutions of the European Union. But they are also rooted in a range of Blairite constitutional reforms. Nigel has become one of a raft of political and judicial watchdogs tasked with policing the government and public life.

How will he feel when people congratulate him? Not smug. Nor superior. This Nigel has mellowed and matured. Gone is the hint of arrogance associated with an untried ideology. He has had to come to terms with situations (such as Angela's illness) that just don't make sense. This Nigel remains rooted in Christian community – indeed a major issue during his own pre and post interview period has been the appointment of a new vicar for All Saints Church – but his commitment is less self-conscious.

In his devotional classic, the medieval monk Thomas à Kempis wrote: "For the resolutions of the just depend rather on the grace of God than on their own wisdom; and in Him they always put their trust, whatever they take in hand. For man proposes, but God disposes; neither is the way of man in his own hands".[7] Nigel would surely have shared in that sentiment. He has always believed in a divine ordering of his path through life. Of course he'll value and keep the letters of congratulation. But it is with the confident yet non-triumphal heart of one 'under orders' that he embraces the happy news of his success.

—⁂—

The setting the BBC's Broadcasting House, Belfast. The date is 1 October 2003. For the next few months the newsroom will buzz with bulletins on IRA decommissioning, on local elections, on power-sharing deals (or the absence of them), but today the focus is on the rights of children.

Nigel stands waiting in the foyer.

With a gentle ping, steel lift doors open.

Enter a production assistant, hand outstretched.

"Commissioner Williams – please come through."

Commissioner Williams! The title is startling. No-one has ever called him that before. Indeed the moment pulsates with firsts: the first day of the month, the first time he's been addressed as Children's Commissioner, his first media interview in his new role which is in itself a first for Northern Ireland.

Outside the studio the first leaves of autumn drift and fall. Nigel has spent the summer tying up the loose ends of a full and fulfilling season of his life. Accompanied by Elizabeth, he has made a final trip to New Zealand, New South Wales and Singapore. He has given Childnet away – into the hands of a natural and able successor, Stephen Carrick-Davies. He has attended the graduation ceremonies of both Simon and Kathryn; seen a new vicar, Frog Orr-Ewing (yes, the man really is called Frog – a nickname that stuck!), inducted into All Souls Church. He has stood by the grave of Heather's sister Angela who, nine years after the initial stroke and heart attack which left her comatose, had finally died.

Now, on the threshold of a whole new era, the microphones are pointed towards him and the cameras whirr. From the BBC studio he moves on to a conference in the Stormont Hotel where he unveils 'NICCY',[7] the pert, black and white border collie, with its 'watchdog' bone, which will be the new trademark logo of his office. At that same conference he sets out his 'watchdog' stall, announcing a major research project to audit Northern Ireland's performance against the United Nation Convention on the Rights of the Child. Throughout the day his voice is heard on every news programme. Again and again he stresses the importance of listening to children, the need "to get past the rhetoric of adults to the realities of their lives."[8]

By the time he returns to his small temporarily rented flat, the stars are out, his back is aching and his ear accustomed to the 'Commissioner Williams' mode of address. Today's round of appointments has included thirteen media interviews and speaking engagements pepper his diary for the month ahead.

It's been exhilarating to be the centre of attention and see people recording his words. But this first day ends as it began with a sobering thought. Words are all very well but Nigel wants action. That morning, reading through Ecclesiastes – a book which offers a comprehensive, if not exactly cheery perspective on life - he had been waylaid by a verse. In the evening he notes it emphatically in his diary: "For in many dreams and in many words there is emptiness. Rather, fear God." (Ecc 5:7)

NOTES

1) From Monday 17 February (2003 diary).

2) From Sunday 22 July (2001 diary).

3) The Belfast Agreement (also known as the Good Friday Agreement) was signed in Belfast on 10 April 1998 (Good Friday) by the British and Irish Governments and was endorsed by most Northern Ireland political parties. Its main provisions included: a recognition of the principle of consent and commitment by all parties to peaceful and democratic methods of achieving constitutional change; the establishment of a Northern Ireland Assembly with devolved legislative powers, of a power-sharing Northern Ireland executive and of a North-South Ministerial Council. Some of its most contentious aspects dealt with the conditional early release of paramilitary prisoners and the establishment of a two year time frame for the decommissioning of paramilitary weapons. The Agreement also included the introduction of legislation governing policing, human rights and equality in Northern Ireland.

4) From Tuesday 13 May (2003 diary).

5) From Thursday 10 April (2003 diary).

6) Thomas à Kempis, *Imitation of Christ*.

7) NICCY stands for Northern Ireland Commissioner for Children and Young people. Nigel recalled that one of the first decisions he took was to substitute the acronym for the full title, on the basis that it was more child-friendly.

8) From the speech Nigel delivered at the 'Towards a better future' conference in the Stormont Hotel, 1 October 2003.

CHAPTER TWENTY

PATIENCE WARD

How is it that the unforeseen can look so maddeningly self-evident in hindsight? Up until late March of the following year nobody, least of all Nigel himself, imagined that he was ill.

For the six months following his appointment, the new Children's Commissioner revelled in his work. Three weekends in four he returned, like a homing pigeon, to Talfourd Road. But the rest of his time was spent in Northern Ireland, focused on the needs of children and young people. He missed his family of course. Still this short-term arrangement allowed Elizabeth to complete her A-level course without disruption. And if pangs of loneliness struck, Nigel could always nip across the street to call in on longstanding family friends, John and Helen Kyle.[1]

John recalls return visits to Nigel's 'bachelor pad'. In the late evening he would find his friend surrounded by books and papers, umbilically attached to his computer – always reading, always thinking – about the provision (or more accurately the lack of provision) for young people with mental health problems, about the problem of young people and paramilitary violence. Against the political backdrop of an Assembly still in suspended animation, Nigel wrestled with these and other macro issues whilst erecting an entire organisation from scratch.

On the NICCY website[2], I find the official report of those first six months in office.[3] Written in his limpid, unstuffy prose, it shows how much ground he covered in that short space of time. The account begins with a passing reference to over two hundred official engagements. Then comes the story of his search for "the right offices in the right place with the right design" – a search which leads him to a prime city centre location (and sees him ruffle the composure of certain civil service suits with off-the-wall requests for plasma screens and circular rooms with multi-coloured walls.) This property search goes hand in hand with a people search as he looks for "the best staff" to support him. By Christmas his Chief Operating Officer, Barney McNeany, has been appointed and the rest of the senior management team is in place by the end of March. The same six month period sees the establishment of policies, procedures and financial and IT systems, together with development of a business plan and its approval by the Office of the First and Deputy First Minister.

Interwoven through all this activity is the silver strand of consultation. At every turn Nigel looks to the group of teenagers involved in his appointment. Result A – a genuinely child-friendly image. Result B – an ethos in which young people feel free to contact him. In those first six months one hundred and twenty-seven individuals ask for his support and from the outset Nigel adopts a two-pronged approach in response. On the one hand he gives specific help in the most difficult cases, whilst on the other, he initiates a range of research projects[4] designed to promote the rights of children across the board.

Spring 2004 brought family developments. In her own colourful style Lynda vaulted off the back of the leap year into the arms of longstanding boyfriend Malcolm who readily said "yes" to her "will you marry me?" (After all, he'd assumed that they would marry all along). Elizabeth set her sights on studying natural science in Cambridge; and their father identified two very different but equally attractive possible homes in Northern Ireland.

House one was large, beautifully restored and located in the leafy environs of Castlewellan. Nigel describes it as having "Lots of character and space. Extensive grounds and buildings," and "Much potential if one was going to run something from home…"

Option two was "a compact house on the Antrim coast. Warm, inviting, homely. Easy to maintain. Beautiful view… lovely gardens… A place to get away from it all…"[5] He booked flights for Heather, Simon and Elizabeth to come over the week before Easter for a family viewing.

—※—

Towards the end of March Nigel enjoyed a happy, relaxed evening with the Kyles. The food was good. The conversation flowed. Still Helen had a niggling concern. "If you ask me, Nigel's lost weight. He must be working too hard… neglecting himself."

Her husband, a medical doctor, nodded thoughtfully. Aware that his friend had been plagued with lower back pain (a recurrent problem that has dogged him over the years) John had not suspected anything sinister but that evening Nigel had mentioned that the pain was keeping him awake at nights. This, John reckoned, called for further investigation. However in the next few days Nigel was off to London.

As far as he was concerned the pain was a tedious blot in on an otherwise fascinating landscape – a nuisance (especially at three in the morning) but one he did his best to ignore. Every so often he refers to it – factual entries without a trace of self pity. "About 3-4 hours sleep last night max," he notes on St Patrick's day. "Split into three periods immediately after medication. I am just so stiff!" What he does not say is that, deprived of the work outlet, he had spent the whole holiday sitting alone in his flat watching rugby, feeling miserable, taking huge doses of Ibrufon and propping himself up to sleep. The following Wednesday he mediates on Psalm 100, 'Sit at my right hand until I make your enemies a footstool for your feet.'

"There is a need to wait," he comments. "Where? With God, at his right hand until the victory comes. I have a lot of pain in my back. It is a real enemy at night. But I need to wait until relief comes. Also I have to rule in the middle of this pain…."[6]

This cast iron determination saw him through the official demands of that final week of the month. He was able to get himself to the airport and fly home. But come Sunday evening he finally gave in. Now on top of chronic back ache and sleeplessness, he had shivering and nausea. He was clearly too unwell to return to Belfast.

—⁓—

On the Tuesday of Holy Week Nigel had an appointment with his doctor. Lynda and Malcolm dropped him off at the surgery, then made their way to Heathrow for their flight to Zimbabwe to visit Malcolm's parents. The previous day Heather, Elizabeth and Simon had travelled to Belfast to look at houses.

Stretched out on the raised leather couch, Nigel expected the usual questions… the usual procedures… For once, though, the GP seemed more concerned with his stomach than his back.

There was a prodding, a pushing, a pursing of lips. "How long has your abdomen been swollen?"

"Swollen! Is it really?" Nigel digested this piece of information with interest.

"Yes," the doctor lifted the phone. "I'm booking you in for an ultrasound."

It wasn't until Nigel saw the expression on the radiologist's face that the truth hit him – this was serious stuff. These suspicions were confirmed when his doctor actually appeared on the doorstep that evening.

"I just wanted to talk to you about your results."

They sat down in the front room. Again Nigel read the body language – direct gaze, sympathetic eyes – and steeled himself.

"The ultrasound showed a large mass round your kidneys."

A mass? The word sounded deliberately neutral, like 'an incident' or 'an episode'.

"It'll take a CT scan to tell us what's really going on but, to be honest, things don't look good."

Alone once again Nigel telephoned the news through to Kathryn in Newcastle and Heather in Northern Ireland, then flopped down in a chair. What do you do when almost out of the blue your whole world is turned upside down? After all, if a doctor admits things don't look good they *really* must be bad. Nigel's diary entry is a classic illustration of his ability to compartmentalise anxiety and avoid panic. "A bit numb by the news," he notes. "Chelsea beat Arsenal which took my mind off things."[7]

—⁓—

Next morning NICCY's recently appointed Chief Operating Officer received a disconcerting phone-call. "Look, Barney," said the voice at the other end of the line. "I don't know what this means. But it sounds as if I won't be back for a while…"

Typically the speaker had already extracted two positives from the wretched development. The first was its timing. Nigel felt relieved that he had had just long enough to appoint his full complement of senior staff. Secondly he felt confident that he'd employed people with the ability and initiative to get on with the job.

—⁓—

Over the next ten days, step by diagnostic step, the physical meaning of the ominous mass on the ultrasound became clear. Maundy Thursday began with a CT scan. Careful positioning. Long minutes alone with the whirr of the machine. Then – action stations – the metaphorical human finger came down on emergency button. "His kidneys are failing." The patient was hustled off into the high dependency renal unit in Guy's Hospital. After a ghastly night (where he later recalled one doctor's peremptory demand for "a very sharp knife"), a visit from an oncology specialist, brought a certain amount of information ("it's cancer") and the promise of more ("we should have the full picture this time next week"). Later that day – Good Friday – he was moved to the fifteenth floor, to the renal unit's Patience Ward.

By this stage in the diagnostic process Nigel had faced the range of possible physical outcomes. His key question was "is this something that will kill me in a short space of time or is this something I'll live with?" That Friday, as Heather, Kathryn, Peter, Simon and Elizabeth accompanied him to his new ward, Frog, the vicar of All Saints, and his wife Amy came to visit. Frog chose to read Psalm 91 – a psalm which had been very significant for Nigel over the years. The words of the opening verse were particularly meaningful. 'He who dwells in the shelter of the Most High will rest in the shadow of the Almighty,'[8] At the start of this week of intense uncertainty, Nigel pictured himself in the shadow of God's presence, as he later put it, "moving with what God was doing – unconditionally."

Easter Sunday 2004

From his fifteenth floor window Nigel watches the sun rise over Canary Wharf, bathing the city in a golden radiance. The whole panorama seems charged with a spiritual energy. Awed, uplifted, he finds himself thinking, "Jesus is alive. Jesus is the person who has totally transformed my life. He's the one I can trust for these circumstances. Depending on which way this goes it may mean a shorter time on earth – and a longer time in heaven."

―∞―

And now it's the Friday of Easter week and his last full day in Patience Ward. Despite ongoing physical discomfort, he has enjoyed life – particularly visits from family and friends and Lynda and Malcolm's return.

"I am so glad that in general I don't feel fear," he writes that morning. "And today is the day for news of the biopsy."[9]

Finally at 5.30 pm the Consultant and the Registrar arrive at his bedside. Afterwards Nigel cannot remember their precise words but the general message has all the clarity of battering ram. His cancer is highly unusual, treatable but incurable. He asks "how long have I got?" The answer: without treatment, weeks; with treatment "months – could go to a year."

―∞―

No matter how prepared you think you are, nobody can really know how they would react to news like that. Without hesitation Nigel opts for the treatment that will allow him to live with cancer, albeit, if the doctors are correct, for a relatively short time. At an emotional level, his immediate response is to reach out to those he loves. When the doctors leave, he clings to his family and breaks the news to his closest friends.

"Small cell cancer – months to live – we cried together – called Simon, L(ynda), E(lizabeth) and M(alcolm) to come in – I managed to explain – more tears! But enjoyed a hug with each of the children. Spoke to Victoria. Spoke to David. H(eather) spoke to a few friends too. H(eather) stayed the night which was brilliant."[10]

That weekend he wrote an email for more general circulation:

Nigel has been diagnosed with an unusual form of small cell cancer in the retroperitoneal space, ie the back of the abdomen. There is no guaranteed medical cure for this condition and life expectancy is hard to predict but is likely to be measured in months…

The news is obviously hard to bear, and we are struggling as a family to come to terms with it. However, Nigel and Heather are convinced that 'his times are in God's hands'. We have not ruled out a miracle but that is not for us to take but for God to give. Please pray with us and rejoice for each breath our God gives.

Periodically, over the next two years, similar emailed 'Health Updates' were sent out – all written with the same factual openness and spiritual hope. Indeed it is interesting to note that one of Nigel's strongest reflex reactions to the crisis was to write. On the Sunday after his diagnosis he notes: "I have had an idea I might write a book – autobiographical but with a challenge… especially if I find it difficult to get back to work."[11]

He also turned to his diary. Before his illness, it was normal for him to let weeks or even months slip by without noting anything, but from the week of his cancer diagnosis right up until days before he died, he celebrated life by recording it – feelings, thoughts, meditations on Scripture, activities, events, rugby and football results.

These entries are very different to the carefully weighed words of the printed emails. They are scribbled (often impossible to decipher), private... raw. He does not dwell on his frustration or his pain but neither does he gloss over them. Here he reveals his dark and vulnerable times: for the fact is that whilst he faced his mortality with remarkable equanimity, he still very much wanted to live.

—⁂—

Living for Nigel had always been bound up with action and giving. On the 23 April, he left hospital with a first chemotherapy session under his belt. The following Friday a McMillan nurse called Veronica came to see him.

"She spent two hours here and learnt the whole story," Nigel notes. "All about family, my history, interests..."[12]

Years earlier, far from home and battered by physical illness, he had been asked a hard question by a Moroccan missionary. "Why are you not thinking of going back and living a true Christian life in a divided society?" His answer to that question had propelled him home to Northern Ireland and set the course for the next ten years of his life.

Now in the privacy of the family lounge, this empathetic nurse has an equally challenging question to put to him – a question which will help him set his course for the months ahead. A caring listener, Veronica has heard all about CARE, Childnet, the Children's Commissioner's role, about Nigel's love of the arts, gardening, travel and sport, about his soul-mate Heather and the children. She knows his medical prognosis of "a year at best", and at the end of it all she simply asks, "What do you hope for now?"

What *does* he hope for now? Nigel searches his heart. The first part of the answer is easy. "Time," he says. But an unspoken "time for what?" hangs between them. How will he spend his days? What is he to do?

Minutes tick past, tears well up, his voice breaks. "Time to walk

Lynda down the aisle... Time to make more of a contribution in Northern Ireland... Time to move back."

NOTES

1) Having moved to London in the early eighties, the Kyles had moved back to Belfast in 1993.

2) www.niccy.org

3) 'Getting Started – First Phase Development of the Northern Ireland Commissioner for Children and Young People, October 2003–March 2004', Annual Report 2003-2004.

4) These research projects include a ambitious project looking at how Northern Ireland meets international agreements on children and young people's rights; a review of vetting procedures for people in contact with children, in the light of the Soham murder case; and a proposal to create a symposium on youth suicide.

5) From Wednesday 10 March (2004 diary).

6) From Wednesday 24 March (2004 diary).

7) From Tuesday 6 April (2004 diary).

8) Psalm 91:1.

9) From Friday 16 April (2004 diary).

10) Ibid.

11) From Sunday 18 April (2004 diary).

12) From Friday 30 April (2004 diary).

CHAPTER TWENTY ONE

ANYTHING YOU WANT

NIGEL'S WISH TO WALK Lynda down the aisle was never fulfilled. Instead he got something even better. On a warm July afternoon he stepped out, a radiant Lynda on his arm, to walk her down a flower-bordered path. She and Malcolm exchanged their vows in a beautiful Suffolk garden and her father had more than enough energy to give an affectionate, witty speech and dance with her at the evening reception.

Further fulfilment lay ahead. Just before his cancer diagnosis Nigel had viewed two properties in Northern Ireland. As the months went by and he emerged from the tunnel of chemotherapy, renting one of them became feasible. "The compact house on the Antrim Coast" would be his and Heather's new home – a home in an Ulster valley, wreathed in birdsong, surrounded by green fields, small villages, rocky wave-lapped beaches, a welcoming local church and a network of peaceful country roads. That August he rejoiced in a resurgence of vigour and in the prospect of this move.

"I feel like I have <u>ESCAPED</u> out of the snare of cancer and ill health for a purpose – of my new job in NI," he wrote[1], "O the freedom – the opportunity to take in gulps of fresh air… to fly like an eagle over the land and see the issues that need to be addressed…" Returning to the office in September, his pleasure in reaching this milestone far exceeded any natural qualms. "First day back in the office. A great feeling. And there was a wonderful buzz with a meeting on prevention of suicide… enjoyed doing a speech. People v(ery) warm and friendly. Spent rest of morning getting on top of appointments…"[2]

The next ten weeks saw him take a demanding programme of events and activities in his stride. Some highlights included meeting with the NICCY Youth Panel ("very lively bunch of young people with very good views"[3]), a robust defence of the Children's Commissioner's role to a group of sceptical school principals ("a lovely day to finish the week with… a good group… they asked lots of questions"[4]) visiting his old school, Portadown College, for the annual speech day ("Very enjoyable… met Jackie Mulligan and Derek Wilson… very little changed"[5]), a trip to Cardiff for a meeting of ENOC, the European Network of Ombudspeople for Children ("ran around at lunchtime organising a statement…"[6]) and launching the 'Your Shout' consultation process[7] on NICCY's fourteen draft priorities. (We were up very early – 5.30 am and left the house at 7.00am… Rehearsals – interviews and then it happened. Went very well. Only technical hitch was when the UTV Live piece didn't come on as planned… I blamed sabotage by the BBC technicians! [8])

Friday 10 December began with a 7.00 am BBC interview on the budget. There followed a radio phone-in on the subject of paramilitary beatings. "Nigel was not one to stay in his comfort zone," his Deputy, Barney McNeeny, recalls. "He gave a strong and positive lead on many contentious issues – not least on the issue of paramilitary violence towards young people." In the previous twelve months there had been a number of serous incidents: the shooting and beating up of a fourteen-year-old boy in New Lodge, North Belfast; the kidnapping, beating and shooting of a seventeen-year-old in West Belfast; the shooting of a sixteen-year-old in East Belfast. Both loyalist and republican paramilitaries had been implicated and Nigel publicly condemned such actions across the board. At the same time, it was a measure of his professional courage that he never passed up the opportunity to go in person to visit organisations or groups from either side of the sectarian divide, including those from whom he might have expected to encounter hostility.

"For me the test is simple," he would say in an official speech later that day. "When my term is up, will I be able to look in the eyes of the young people involved in my recruitment and say to them, 'I defended your rights and I achieved change on your behalf'?"

The test might have been simple but the job certainly wasn't. Nigel's official remit was broad, with much room for overlap and treading on toes. He faced an array of stakeholders, most of whom naturally saw 'critical' and 'friend' as a contradiction in terms, in a country where the very mention of 'rights' provoked diverse reactions. The Commissioner needed to educate, challenge, hold to account, threaten, persuade, disarm, charm, discern, budget, reach out, seize the moment, play, earn respect, listen, understand and communicate with the widest variety of audiences.

Some might ask, and no doubt did, how Nigel reconciled his evangelical faith with a role within a 'rights culture' of tolerance, diversity and inclusion which at certain points, particularly in the area of human sexuality, cut across traditional Christian morality. The answer lay to some extent in his pragmatism. But also in a profoundly Christian understanding of what it meant to love his neighbour – whoever they were, whatever they believed. In a world where many had lost the sense of a moral imperative to care, Nigel saw human rights legislation as a means of levering 'the haves' into those million and one imperceptible movements of heart, mind and will that can improve life for the 'have nots.'

Still he carried an inner tension. In one of his sabbatical poems, a piece called 'The Secret One', he had explored the tightrope walked by those with deep religious convictions operating in the secular sphere. His subject was Joseph of Arimathea, a first century district counsellor look-alike, who initially kept his Christian discipleship under wraps, but then went public, asking Pilate for permission to bury the crucified Jesus in his family tomb.

> He was torn, schizophrenic
> Should he declare his allegiance
> Show solidarity and identify
> With people he would normally loathe?
> Or should he stay camouflaged
> Allowing his true self
> To be disguised by respectable
> Greens and browns...

It is interesting to see how Nigel resolves this tension in a powerful closing stanza.

> Secrecy is not bad
> The purists say "Hypocrisy!"
> The foolhardy say "Cowardice!"
> But the wise say
> "Exploit the hidden to confound the exposed."[9]

Again in a diary note on Christian witness he writes: "'Let your light shine before men in such a way that they see your good works and glorify your father who is in heaven' – I think it is very important to focus on 'in such a way'... I still feel it means don't blind people. Don't confuse people. Shine your light on the evil and not in people's eyes... But I am very concerned this does not become a cop out. I won't shine in case I offend someone sort of thing."[10] Clearly he lived with the awareness that his public position generally offered the opportunity to exert a strategic influence for good from within the system but that there might well be specific issues where he would have to come out on a moral or ethical limb.

If a readiness to speak out and an even-handed courage were two characteristics which the Children's Commissioner displayed in his approach to his job, the commemorative collages on the wall of the Nigel Williams Conference Room in the NICCY offices perfectly capture a third. All show Nigel surrounded by children. Strikingly in two of them he is perched on a desk, a diminutive leprechaun figure, interacting with life-size children. The civil servant who once perched cross-legged on filing cabinets had become a dignitary who regularly bounded up steps two at a time, never passed up the opportunity to engage with a football, scrabble-board, pool table, Xbox or a plain old bucket and spade, and could have gleefully declaimed the satiric lines: "People must not do things for fun. We are not here for fun. There is no reference to fun in any Act of Parliament"[11]. There was an exuberant, irrepressible child in him always eager to break out and play.

Imagine his pleasure, then, when he came into the office on 20 January to find his desk festooned with balloons and a banner wishing him a happy 50th birthday. "Later Pat interrupted us and took me to the corridor where I was sure she was going to tell me about a difficult case but in fact it was for a surprise cake and coffee!" he records. "What a team! What good fun!" And it didn't stop there. The week before his official party – the occasion of a meticulously planned and road-tested treasure hunt – Heather whisked him off to a hotel in Limavady for a luxury weekend with the Kyles and the Alexanders, (smuggled into the country for the occasion). The thing that most delighted him about this was the way, like the staff, she managed to fool him into expecting something completely different.

In the middle of February Nigel had a hospital appointment. The seventeenth of the month was the date of his first scan of the New Year. Medical reports up until that point had been quite encouraging. After his initial course of chemotherapy, the tumour in his abdomen had shrunk considerably though it had not completely gone away. A further scan in Belfast at the beginning of November was also reassuring.

That Thursday he and Heather rose early. By coincidence, their morning Bible reading was on Jesus' teaching about worry. 'But if God clothes the grass of the field which is alive today and tomorrow is thrown into the furnace, will he not much more clothe you, O ye of little faith.' [12]

"This is having faith in the sense of trusting God… faith rather than fear," Nigel wrote in his diary. "A simple confidence and belief that God is God and it's no use worrying about the situation that we are in. A quiet trust – not brash or overbearing,"

He presented himself to the radiographer in an optimistic frame of mind. He felt in good shape. After his November report of a "well-diminished tumour and no sign of any cancer elsewhere", he was hopeful that his condition had remained stable. But the morning would bring a crushing blow.

"Mr H met me after the scan and said there had been real deterioration on the left side and I would need more chemo," he records. "H was upset. I was surprised… No predictions on life expectancy. Hopefully at least six months…"[13]

Some weeks earlier, on the last day of the old year, Nigel had taken time out to reflect. He'd sensed ten simple words of direction: "Be yourself, give yourself, pace yourself, be restored, give yourself."[14] Now in the wake of the consultant's grim news, this is what he does. He gives himself – going into the office to explain the situation to Pamela, his PA and the rest of the staff before picking up a family friend from the airport. Next morning, he paces himself – does not head out first thing into the rush hour traffic. After breakfast again he gives himself – this time to writing a key-note speech for a forthcoming conference. Drawing on a deep inner well of awareness and concern, he sits down and types away. "Got really into the flow and had it done by 10.30 am," he notes.[15]

–––∿∿∿–––

The Hope Conference[16] for which that speech was written took place four days later. It had been organised by NICCY to promote action in the whole area of mental health, addressing in particular the tragic problem of suicide and self-harm. That morning Nigel stepped up to the lectern to address a richly diverse audience – a mix of over 200 young people and professionals. The speech he gave was published in full in *The Independent* the following Friday and contains the following words.

"I… have a dream for the children and young people of Northern Ireland. I have a dream that you will not be stressed out by the academic pressures of school and the need to perform.

"I have a dream that the hoods in our society who control whole neighbourhoods with intimidation, threats and punishments will leave young people alone and that the drugs trade they largely control will be eradicated.

"I have a dream that anyone who is bullied will be immediately supported in their school or youth group, that bullying will not be tolerated, and no young person will feel desperate and alone because of other's threats.

"I dream of a day when we have a clear strategy for child and adolescent mental health that includes promotion, prevention, community care and acute care.

"A day when there is no rivalry between professionals in the community and those who provide acute psychiatric care; a day when we have the highest ratio in the UK of professional psychiatrists to young patients rather than one of the lowest.

"I dream of a Northern Ireland where every school has some counselling provision whether provided by an outside agency or a trained staff member; where every child has someone to turn to when the going gets tough; where funding for such services is mainstreamed, guaranteed, and sufficient.

"I dream of a place where no child, save for the most exceptional circumstances, has to leave Northern Ireland to get the professional help they need."

He went on to make a plea for the kind of determined, co-ordinated response that could realise this vision.

Some months later, while he was in hospital receiving chemotherapy, he recieved a telephone call from a government minister, to whom he'd written with a 'needs of children' shopping list. The politician had been, as Nigel puts it, "very surprised to learn that I was in hospital and very warm and funny about it."[16]

"Under the circumstances you can have anything you want," the minister joked.

It's a telling response. In a free society where speakers and preachers regularly call for change, words so often make the same kind of non-impression as mood music. Two factors, can add to their impact. One is the context in which the words are spoken and the other the background experience of the speaker.

People are inclined to hear differently when they know that

words are spoken by someone who has earned the right to speak them. "Be yourself," Nigel had written in his diary. On the morning of the Hope Conference, *who* he was – a man whose passion to make a difference had caused him to devote what he knew potentially to be the last twelve months of his life to meeting the needs of children and young people – must surely, even in hindsight, add weight to what he said.

NOTES

1) From Thursday 19 August (2004 diary).
2) From Monday 20 September (2004 diary).
3) From Monday 27 September (2004 diary).
4) From Friday 8 October (2004 diary).
5) From Friday 22 October (2004 diary).
6) From Wednesday 13 October (2004 diary).
7) The fourteen draft priorities were based on findings emerging on the QUB research project, looking at how Northern Ireland compared to the international standard of the United Nations Convention on the Rights of the Child. After consultation a fifteenth priority was added to the list.
8) From Monday 18 October (2004 diary).
9) From 'The Secret One', 29 July 2002.
10) From Thursday 13 January (2005 diary).
11) AP Herbert, *Uncommon Law*, Methuen, 1935, p28.
12) Matthew 6:30
13) From Thursday 17 February (2005 diary).
14) From Friday 31 December (2004 diary).
15) From Friday 18 February (2005 diary).
16) The HOPE conference, organised by NICCY on mental health and the prevention of self-harm and suicide, was held in the Park Avenue Hotel, Belfast on 22 February 2005.
17) From Wednesday 20 July (2005 diary).

CHAPTER TWENTY TWO

THE FINAL MOVE

ONE THING MOST PEOPLE in Nigel's state of health would not choose to do is pack up and move the entire contents of their home. Yet in April 2005 this is exactly what he and Heather did. That spring 14 Talfourd Road was sold. At last they were in a position to take possession of the rented house in the valley which they had already begun to consider their own. For the past seven months they had gloried in seeing the sun rise over the sea from the bedroom window. Morning after morning Heather had walked down to the shore to sit on a large rock and watch the waves roll in. They had spent Saturdays out in the surrounding countryside, exploring its forests and waterfalls, delighting in the variety of local birdlife.

This was a home into which they had already welcomed many guests and would welcome many more. Idwal and Sheila, Sue and David, Larry and Patti Magid, Steve Carrick-Davies, the Prestons, the Wilsons (remember it was in their family kitchen that Nigel and Heather met) Margaret, John, Claire and Norma (from Portadown College days) were just a few of the friends and relatives who passed through their door.

The Williams called their property *Sea Braes*[1] and had the name carved out on a name board. But in a heart-rending diary entry Nigel refers to his tears of frustration at not having the energy to go out and hang it up. Chemotherapy had engulfed him "in a great marshmallow of tiredness." [2] Low moments such as this, however, were not at all typical of his general attitude. At the beginning of the year he had made the following note in his diary, based on the verse from Matthew's Gospel: "Blessed are those who mourn for they shall be comforted."[3]

"The implication of this is that mourning is a good thing to do. H thinks this is about more than death. Perhaps the blessing comes because you are coming to terms with a situation through mourning. So that… the person who mourns is in a better place than the one who doesn't. I have mourned my own loss of health but I cannot stay mourning…"[4]

In many ways the move from Talfourd Road to *Sea Braes* could be seen as the outworking of this irrepressible hope and determination to keep living life to the full. An excerpt from an email written on the day life returned to normal shows how he coped with clearing out, packing up and transporting furniture from place to place.

9 April 2005

The past week has been a major feat of organisation, masterminded by Heather. We initially had to pack all our belongings in the Glenarm house, so that the landlords could come and move their furniture out. Then Heather travelled to London to pack up the belongings in our house there before returning to Glenarm today to unpack everything which had arrived from London, and those boxes we had left behind.

Our four children have been fantastic in giving their help – Lynda and her hubbie Malcolm were able to be with Heather all week at each stage. Simon was off on Thursday and Friday to help in London and then travel here; and Kathryn came off night duty at midnight and flew here this morning to help with the unpacking. Meanwhile Elizabeth was my carer in chief, as she and I moved to

our good friends John and Helen Kyle's home in Belfast
for the week, and avoided all the hustle and bustle.

In April 1983, twenty-three years previously (almost to the day)
Nigel had noted the following 'prophetic' message in his journal:

> *You will be sent out*
> *To help change this country*
> *To bring my words of life…*
>
> *You will have to work for it*
> *It will not come easily*
> *And you'll need your family.*

Let's step outside the back door of rationalism for a moment.
Let's take a deep breath and accept (even briefly) that people really
do sometimes hear God speak. Then let's ask a very basic question.
How do you know whether a prophecy is genuine, self-fulfilling
or the product of a fevered imagination?

As an unqualified layperson, skating blithely over ice-flows of
doctrine, I have four simple suggestions. A real message proves
itself through time; it is not usually widely recognised; it hits home
with the glass-shattering accuracy of a perfectly pitched note; it
often comes to pass in an unexpected manner.

You'll need your family. From April 2004 Nigel needed his
family in a way he could never have foreseen. Without them he
simply could not have moved back to Northern Ireland and done
what he did. That spring he meditated on persevering under trial.
"I think I now have a little, not a lot, but a little understanding
of what this means," he writes "with having to fight cancer and
keep on at my job, and life. But for me this is not a picture of an

197

isolated man fighting against the odds, but of a team surrounding me and supporting me and cheering me on."[5] Despite her personal heart-break, Heather in particular, supplied the devoted care that allowed Nigel to keep playing a role he loved.

Towards the end of May Nigel's friends received an upbeat email.

24 May 2005

Hi everyone

Some good news to share! I had my CT scan yesterday after the first four sessions in my current course of chemotherapy.

This showed that the cancer tumour had reduced to about half the size it was before the treatment started. Also, some spots of secondary cancer on my liver and chest had disappeared.

My consultant has suggested that I should receive a further four sessions of chemotherapy rather than the two more originally planned. This will take the chemotherapy through until August, and mean we will need to adjust our holiday plans. However, this is a small price to pay when we know the new chemotherapy is working effectively against the cancer.

So Heather and I are rejoicing in this good news…

But, four months later hopes were dashed once again.

4 October 2005

Hi there!

I had sent out a general update on my health in May, shortly after a CT scan had shown my cancer tumour had reduced substantially after the first half of my second course of chemotherapy. I completed this chemo in

August and it is fair to say that the side effects got more pronounced as the course progressed. I am still dealing with pins and needles in my feet, which may take some months to wear off.

But overall I am feeling much better, and enjoyed a great holiday with Heather wedged between two chemo sessions... Work has also gone well, with a very demanding schedule of appointments in September, including a three day trip to Warsaw for a European meeting of Commissioners & Ombudsmen for Children.

It was therefore a real shock last week when a further CT scan showed that the tumour had grown again, was bigger than in May, and that a secondary spot on the liver had become 'more defined'. The consultant suggested that another course of chemotherapy with a different drug might be possible, but warned of potential side effects and uncertain benefits.

After a lot of thought, prayer and conversations within our family I have decided not to seek further chemo at this time. I am not closing the door on treatment, nor feeling that I have reached a point of inevitable decline! Rather, I feel at peace about continuing to give the most I can to life, and especially in my role as Commissioner for Children and Young People. I hope to have a further scan in due course.

Heather and I are trusting God in this new adventure and challenge...

By this stage Nigel was enjoying what he personally considered to be the most fruitful period in his new role since the six months immediately after his appointment. The previous day he and his

staff had celebrated NICCY's second birthday with a cake bought
by Nigel for the occasion. Other than that, the anniversary had
been filled with the activities he routinely undertook to ensure
that young people's needs were taken into account and their voices
heard. In the afternoon, for example, he'd travelled to Limavady
to meet with a member of the youth panel and plan a presentation
they would make to the Association of Chief Police Officers the
following week. No doubt it would have been easier simply to
go and make the presentation himself – but that had never been
Nigel's way.

—⁓—

Cut to Barbados. The setting is a small boutique hotel on the
beach. Heather and Nigel have flown there for a ten day, mid-
autumn break. Picture them facing each other across a low table
out of the glare of the afternoon sun. Sense the tension in the air.
Heather avoids eye contact, staring out to sea, brow furrowed.
Nigel waits intently for her to make the next move. No, it isn't
a domestic! They are engaged in a fiercely competitive game of
scrabble.

"Heather crushed me in our usual game of scrabble." Nigel
notes in his diary that evening. "I gave her a 50 point start but she
won easily getting a 7 letter word in the process. Maybe it is all
about helping her relax…"[6]

And relax they did. Those were intimate days spent with books,
on sun loungers, round the scrabble board, in the whirlpool,
against the back-drop of a magnificent ocean, spectacular sunsets,
shimmering horizons. "I am normally such an active holiday
person, such a traveller," Nigel remarked. "I have started the
book by Ewan McGregor[7] on his journey round the world on a
motorbike. That is my sort of adventure and he clearly enjoys the

planning, preparing and doing, as do I. So perhaps… this is about an inner journey, an inner adventure which will happen without moving far…"[8]

For Nigel that inner journey became an exploration in the theme of biblical justice which led to what he refers to as a "crafted prayer".

"Father, please help me to give as you have commanded
Use me in my weakness to shame the strong –
the institutions of power and self-interest
Grant me righteous indignation, that will
always be infused with dignity
May I bring justice without partiality
and a compassion for the poor, the orphan,
The abandoned…
So that this triangle of compassion, indignation
and justice will bring change to the lives of many."

And now it's two days to Christmas. In the preceding week Nigel has written cards, celebrated his 27th wedding anniversary, spent a day in Edinburgh meeting with his UK Children's Commissioner counterparts and worked through the usual welter of correspondence. He has also continued to wrestle with the decision of whether or not to undergo a further course of chemotherapy in the New Year.

That Friday morning Heather leaves the house in a rush to pick up Lynda and Malcolm from the airport. "Don't expect us back straight away. We'll be Christmas shopping on the way home," she calls as she dashes out the door. Nigel grins, fondly anticipating the arrival of his middle daughter. "A phenomenal shopper," was how he'd described her on her wedding day. Lynda has a better nose for a bargain than anyone he's ever met. He looks forwards to seeing her burst through the door, garlanded with carrier bags full of enchanting purchases obtained at minimal expense.

Today, however, the return of the shopping party does not follow its predicted course. The bags are there, but, for once, their contents are disregarded. Lynda and Malcolm have news… BIG news…

"As soon as they got back they told us that L(ynda) was pregnant which is <u>very</u> exciting," Nigel records. "I wrote a poem about how I feel about life – the paradox of shadows and sun, confinement and openness."

"I feel at peace in God," he adds on New Year's Eve. "Calm, like my poem said. Physical challenges can throw me off course. But I want to keep going. Moving in God's strength… Stay free – don't let it beat you."

His next email arrived in the second week in January.

11 January 2006

Hi folks

I thought it would be good to update my friends and all those praying for me at the beginning of the New Year.

My last scan was in early December and showed the cancer was continuing to grow, especially the secondary tumours on the lungs and liver. I was offered further treatment with a different drug mix, however the benefits of this treatment while possibly good were very uncertain against the certainty of considerable disruption.

After a lot of thought, prayer and discussion with my family and friends over Christmas, I decided that I would not pursue further treatment at this stage. This was a very difficult decision, but one we do feel at peace about.

My pain levels have increased considerably in the last 6 weeks and the medication has therefore increased to match it. I am a little more tired as a result. I am keen to maintain my work as much as possible, and Heather is being very supportive in seeking to ensure that, eg driving me if I have appointments outside Belfast.

It is a day to day existence, trusting God for the energy and the spiritual and mental strength to keep going, take the decisions I need to and fulfil the job commitments I have.

There have been real encouragements – a wonderful Christmas, a great article profiling my work in the Belfast Telegraph last week; and tomorrow I am travelling to Namur in Belgium to receive an international award for my work with children and technology...

Nigel's diary Friday 13 January
REST. Train to Namur, to hotel. Two interviews by phone. REST. Dressed... then round to lecture theatre. Reception, presentation, lecture – delivered sitting down and questions. A good buzz with the audience. Then back to hotel. REST. Beautiful meal in a lovely Belgian restaurant. Time for bed.

Wedensday 18 January
A very difficult day. Visit to... special school and opening a community centre...

But I was in pain – lots of it. And playing with the kids in the soft play area did not help...

Monday 23 January
Back to work – with a vengeance. I felt full of energy and had good meetings with Barney and Pamela. And then working on a letter to the Office of the First Minister and Deputy First Minister... Then lunch, a rest and busy afternoon with two meetings... and

then the business plan review. H came and picked me up and home in some pain.

Wednesday 25 January

Well I vowed to give myself to today – it did not turn out quite as expected. I prepared my speech for Thursday and then went… to… launch the play policy…

I just managed to get through my speech – a real struggle, and then got H to bring me home… John K came about 10.00 pm. Sounded chest carefully and then advised an X-ray.

13 February 2006

As many of you will know I have been in Belfast City Hospital now for just over two weeks, am likely to be here for some time longer.

I have been struggling with breathlessness, especially at a public speaking engagement where I found it hard to finish my speech. My GP thought I should get checked over, and sure enough some hospital tests showed I had some blood clots on my lungs.

Thus I was admitted to a respiratory ward and given blood thinning drugs to disperse the clots and prevent others forming… I have been up and down and round the houses in hospital both physically and in other ways. I have been in four wards, had three catheters inserted and removed, and coped with excruciating pain and blessed relief.

Overall though, as Heather (who has been my constant companion and had her hand squeezed to the point pain at times) and I have prayed together, we feel a sense of moving towards the end of the dark tunnel and the light is not far away…

One other thing – our son Simon has won a place in the London Marathon and is running for Cancer Research UK… I hope to be in London in April to cheer him on.

—m—

Cut to *Seabraes*. It's a Sunday 26 February. Nigel sits with his friend John Kyle in the bedroom. He got out of hospital four days ago, knowing that a trip to London would be a physical impossibility. So he makes the most of watching sport on TV – an activity which over the last half-an-hour has reduced him to a state of raw anxiety. The Six Nations rugby season is in full flight. Ireland are playing Wales and the Irish are 5-0 down. Happily, during the second half the Irish forwards come into their own. With his team in a comfortable lead Nigel is able to bend his mind to other things. He turns to his GP. "How long have I got?" he inquires.

It's a difficult moment for any medic. Empathetically John searches round for the right words. But even as he's making his carefully hedged pronouncement, the patient loses interest. Nigel's eyes are on the TV screem... on Brian O'Driscoll breaking through a tackle.

"Go... Go... Go! Pass! Yeees!" He punches the air. "What a try!"

"Ireland eventually won 31-5 with some dominant final play and good O'Driscoll leadership," he notes that evening. "John and I had a surreal conversation about my life prospects while watching the second half."

No doubt that Irish victory helped Nigel absorb his medical prognosis without flinching. He knew now that they had entered the end game, for whatever way you hedged it, John's answer to the question "how long have I got?" was essentially "not long."

Nigel's diary Tuesday 28 February

Today was the day staff came out to see me along with Pamela. It was a beautifully bright and crisp winter's day with four seasons in an hour. It was inevitably emotional saying goodbye. There were tears and very warm good wishes.

Saturday 4 March

No time to pray overtly this morning... as we were expecting Lynda Neilands, the potential writer of my biography. Kat and Pete went and picked her up in Belfast. We got into things quite quickly and I talked into the tape... about the coming of the Kingdom of God and the need to influence lives through political and other means.

Lynda is really interested... but it has job implications... We will wait and see what God has for us. But it was excellent to talk over my ideas...

NOTES

1) Brae is the Scottish lowland word for hill.
2) From Saturday 19 March (2005 diary).
3) Matthew 5:4
4) From Saturday 1 January (2005 diary).
5) From Sunday 13 March (2005 diary).
6) From Friday 4 November (2005 diary).
7) Ewan McGregor and Charley Boorman, *Long Way Round*, Time Warner, 2005.
8) From Sunday 30 October (2005 diary).

MARCH 2006

NIGEL AND I TALKED again the following fortnight. On the second visit, he was noticeably weaker but as relaxed and upbeat as ever. Again we savoured the view from the bedroom window; a wintry panorama of fields dotted with what looked like patches of frozen snow until the white kaleidoscope shifted and I realized they were gulls. Beyond, the sea glinted a steely grey and the Mull of Kintyre was shrouded in mist.

He was still keen to think about this book. "I don't want you to rush things," he told me. "If you write it you'll need to get your own perspective. I've kept diaries. But you'll want to talk to other people too."

During the intervening weeks I had spoken to a couple of publishers, one of whom had encouraged me to ask Nigel to reflect on the experience of terminal illness and to make this the thrust of the book. But Nigel wanted to reflect on life not death. He and Kathryn had drawn up a time-line, indicating the tall trees in his life journey – the big decisions, the major events. He believed his experiences could be used to illustrate the positive fruits of principled choices, values and decision-making and he wanted his story to be shared in a way that highlighted the Christian faith which had motivated him throughout. He wanted people, especially those climbing the career ladder, to think about their own motivation; to encourage them to use their talents for the common good.

That morning he tired more quickly than on my previous visit and opted for an early lunch so he could chat a little longer before resting. We said our goodbyes and I stepped outside into a world that had changed. The frost had melted; the sun was out; it was like a last conversation before spring.

Nigel died ten days later – on 28 March. He kept up his diary until the 24 of the month and took pleasure in sport, in the birds that visited his bird table, and in the friends, including his minister the Rev Anne Tolland, who visited him. He was comforted above all by the presence of beloved family. His final, slightly unsteady diary entry contains an appreciative comment on some physiotherapy equipment and a brief reflection on the "orchestra of sound" in the opening verses of Psalm 92.

It ends with an emphatic "Hallelujah!"

EPILOGUE

These are a few of the many postings that flooded the NICCY and Childnet noticeboard after Nigel's death:

"From the moment I clapped eyes on Nigel I knew I wanted to work with him...

He had such an energy and vitality. My son, Ruairi, came to NICCY one day and he told me that, as he was standing at the photocopier helping out, he saw Nigel 'skipping' across the general office from his room to mine, no doubt to get telling me the latest idea he had, the latest networking opportunity he had come across for NICCY, the latest way we could influence policy makers to make children and young people's lives better. That was the way he was, full of energy and ideas and buzz."
Barney McNeany, Chief Executive, NICCY

"He truly was a Champion for Children and Young People doing all he possibly could to ensure we had a better life. Nigel was one in a million and will always be in our hearts."
Claire McCambley, NICCY Youth Panel Member

"I have listened to several international speeches before about the benefits of the Internet, and these were great speeches, but I have seldom been touched in a way I felt when I heard Nigel's speech at the then Cable and Wireless Childnet Awards in England 2003... I was touched by every word he said and coming from Africa, these were words that can help heal the soul even in the face of many challenges in access to the Internet..."
Andrew B Greene, iEARN, Sierra Leone

"...Above all else, Nigel was endlessly curious about life. He was not a single issue guy. He loved his work and he also loved his wife and family and was very proud of them. He served his local community and was amazingly engaged with people on his street, his neighbourhood, local council and right the way up to heady government circles and international institutions. He always seemed to make time for you; he was a great listener and was one of the best at chairing a meeting I have ever met."
Stephen Balkam, CEO, Family Online Safety Institute

"'He is no fool who gives what he cannot keep to gain that which he cannot lose', words from Jim Elliot, a twentith century Christian martyr, and words which inspired Nigel on his life's journey. He had other heroes – CT Studd, Lord Shaftsbury, William Wilberforce, and that most eminent of civil servants, Daniel of the Bible! They reinforced in Nigel a belief that God calls his people to live as light and salt in this world, and to pursue justice and mercy with passion and determination, making a difference in every place they find themselves. And so he has... He has been tireless in his dedication, unflagging in his zeal and, even as he faced the end of this chapter of his life, displayed such a sense of peace and optimism that those of us who observed have been left full of wonder – and worship."
Margaret

"...Nigel fought a good fight. He kept the faith. And now he starts the task for which he trained all his life. The story goes on..."
David and Janet Preston

QUESTIONS FOR PERSONAL REFLECTION OR GROUP DISCUSSION

• Nigel was once described as a 'Coordinating Prime Mover.' What phrase would you use to describe yourself? Where do you find opportunities to realise your gifts and abilities?

• Who has had an encouraging influence on your life and what did they teach you? Are they aware of the impact that they made?

• How open are you to spiritual adventure? Have you friends who will journey with you along the way? What is your view of God, the Church, and the Bible?

• How do you react to challenging questions? Do they make you defensive or are you open to their benefits? Who cares enough to challenge you?

• How do you regard people whose culture/tradition is different to your own? Do the groups you identify with reinforce prejudice or do they confront it?

• How ready are you to work at relationships – especially with those closest to you? Are there folk with whom you can talk honestly about the things that matter to you most?

• What value do you place on comfort and security? How open are you to new initiatives? How ready are you to encourage/ support other people in their ventures?

- What kind of activities take your mind off work and help you keep problems in perspective? Would you say you have a holistic view of life? If you were to map out your priorities for the month ahead, how would the map look?

- To what extent do you dialogue with God? What effect does this have on your life?

- What is your attitude when your life becomes a maelstrom of activity. Do you fight against it, feel overwhelmed by it, or do you enjoy the adrenalin rush of the ride? How strong is your sense of direction?

- How do you handle loss? Have you grieved and come to terms with your disappointments? How have you benefited from such experiences? Are you open to recognising/celebrating your own and other people's success?

- How would you describe your motivation level over the last twelve months? Have there been periods of drifting? How would you spend a sabbatical or career break?

- Have you ever explored a new art form, ie painting, music, creative writing? Could you have a gift in one or more of these areas. Are you open to unwrapping it?

- Have you had a recent experience of change? How did you find it? Do you see a change looming up ahead? How does that make you feel?

- What is the biggest dream you have ever dreamt? What is your biggest dream right now?

- The German poet, Rilke wrote: "God give us each our own death, the dying that proceeds from each of our lives, the way we loved, the meanings we made…" Our lives continually touch and influence the lives of others. What legacies have you received? What legacies do you hope to pass on?

Children's Champion